Country Life Book of

DOGS

S. M. LAMPSON

Illustrations by

BRIDGET OLERENSHAW

THE MACMILLAN COMPANY NEW YORK

First published in the
United States of America by
The Macmillan Company, New York, 1963
Filmset and printed in Great Britain by
Photoprint Plates Ltd., Basildon, Essex

© S. M. Lampson 1963

Library of Congress
Catalog Card Number 63-13534.

Contents

Section 4. Terriers (*page 109*)

Section 5. Non-Sporting (*page 149*)

Foreword

IF we are to understand our dog and his deep-seated instincts and instinctive reactions we must look backwards into the history of his breed and not merely at his immediate background. A pedigree is but a piece of paper which records three, four or five generations of a dog's immediate ancestors: read intelligently there is a great deal to be learnt from it, but not the whole story. For the reason for his physical appearance, his urges and physical and mental characteristics, one must look further back than a mere five generations. Five dog generations can be covered in a mere ten years or even less. A breed history may go back a thousand years or more—admittedly not a line of pure, unsullied blood, but a long period of time during which dogs of the same make and shape have done the same kind of work. Some breeds have become interlaced through being crossed, generally for some specific reason or purpose, and a new breed has emerged with a new slant to its character and changed in build and size. There are few breeds that did not originally have some specific purpose in life, even if it was only to be a pretty, pampered plaything.

The history of dogs is a vast one and in many breeds there are whole stretches of their evolution and development of which no record has been kept. The space available in one book is limited and this one merely sets out to give the reader a glimpse of the background of the various breeds accepted in this country at the present time, with a brief description of their appearance, together with drawings of typical examples of them all. The author and the artist hope that the combination of word and picture will help the reader to appreciate his dog a little better than he did before.

Both the author and the artist would like to thank all those who, by their interest and practical help, have given them so much encouragement. The author would like Mrs Olerenshaw to know how much she admires her charming drawings and to thank her for her enthusiasm, patience and co-operation.

I would also like personally to thank Mr E. Holland Buckley and the Committee of Cruft's Dog Show Society for giving me permission to use the descriptions of breeds as published in Cruft's Catalogue; this ensures that the descriptions are authoritative, even if it has not always been possible to quote them in full.

1963   S. M. LAMPSON

HOUNDS

Afghan Hounds   Basenjis   Basset Hounds

Beagles   Bloodhounds   Borzois

Dachshunds   Deerhounds   Elkhounds

Finnish Spitz   Greyhounds   Irish Wolfhounds

Rhodesian Ridgebacks   Salukis   Whippets

HOUNDS

THE term hound is applied to the types of dog whose fundamental purpose is hunting. At the present time the English Kennel Club recognises and classifies twenty-three different breeds as hounds, but for present purposes Foxhounds, Harriers and Otterhounds have been omitted from this section, for their work is specialised and they are seldom to be found as house or show dogs; the six varieties of Dachshund have been dealt with as one breed since they are twigs of the same branch.

Some of the fifteen varieties of hound which appear in the following pages are of very ancient lineage—the owners of Afghan Hounds who claim that the forefathers of their dogs were taken into the Ark by Noah may not be so very wide of the mark. Both Afghan Hounds and Salukis—which breed is the older is a point that has never been satisfactorily settled—were certainly known in the third millenium B.C. The Deerhound and the Greyhound of the present day differ little from the hounds known and valued by the Greeks, the Romans and the Celts. The great hounds that astonished the Romans when they conquered these islands were probably not dissimilar to the Irish Wolfhounds of today, although a break in their history makes it doubtful whether there is any true line of descent.

By comparison with these ancient types some of the hound breeds we know today may appear parvenus, but period, place and purpose have necessarily produced different types—some built for speed and others for endurance; some hounds hunt mainly by sight, others rely almost entirely on their exquisite powers of scent discrimination. While some hounds hunt in silence others give tongue once they have found their line and their music is greatly esteemed. Some breeds hunt to kill while others are only expected to bring their quarry to bay so that their masters can administer the *coupe de grâce*.

Whatever their breed, size or purpose all hounds have certain physical characteristics in common—deep chests, powerful jaws, strong necks, well-muscled quarters and good legs and feet, to which must be added courage. In character, a hound must have the independence to be able to do his work alone and yet be responsive to his master's call even in the heat of the chase, and their courage must be beyond question.

In this modern world many hounds are never employed to do the work for which they were originally bred, but pass their lives giving companionship to their owners and appear on the show bench. It is, therefore, important that the basic and essential qualities of hound character and appearance should be understood, retained, sustained and appreciated if age-old instincts and capabilities are not to be swamped and lost through disuse.

11

Afghan Hounds

TO claim that there were Afghan Hounds in the Ark may be a flight of fancy, but there can be no doubt that hounds very similar in type, and having the same peculiar high. tail carriage, are depicted in the rock carvings on the walls of the caves of Balkh: these are believed to date from the third millenium B.C.

The Afghan Hound and the Saluki have much in common and the latter was carefully bred and highly valued in ancient Egypt. There can be little doubt that the Afghan and the Saluki are two branches of the same tree; there is no reason, either geographical or historical, why the dogs of Egypt should not have travelled through Arabia into Persia and thence to the mountainous regions of Afghanistan that were for so long inhospitable. It was, in fact, in the one-time Persian province of Bactria, which came under the rule of Afghanistan in 1841 when its name was changed to Balkh, that the cave drawings were discovered.

When Europeans first began to travel in the wild and then largely unknown country of Afghanistan they found that the maliks and governors of the districts were proud of the hounds. These had been carefully bred for centuries for the purpose of hunting wolves and deer as well as for coursing hares and foxes. Not infrequently the smaller game was hunted in conjunction with hawks.

'Shalizada', also known as 'Gazelle', was the first Afghan to be exhibited in this country and arrived about 1894. In 1897 'Dilkoosh', who was described as an Afghan Barakhzy Hound, made an appearance at a show and was followed by several whose names and description make it apparent that, although believed to be pure-bred Afghans, they were more likely to have been sheep dogs of a type common in the mountainous regions of Afghanistan. 'Zardin', who was imported and owned by Captain Barff, made a sensation when he won at the Kennel Club Show in 1907 and was afterwards taken to Buckingham Palace at the request of Queen Alexandra. However, 'Zardin' and his kennel companions came to a mysterious end and no more was heard of the breed in this country for some years.

In 1920 Major and Mrs Bell Murray and Miss Manson brought three dogs and four bitches to this country. These animals aroused considerable interest but, although two or three litters were born, not much progress was made until two major events occurred. Firstly, Mrs Amps brought 'Sirdar of Ghazni' home with her when she returned from Kabul. Sirdar was not only the finest example of his breed yet seen in this country, but he had the power of passing his virtues to his offspring. Secondly, the formation of the Afghan Club centralised the interests of the breed. The result was that the late Mr A. Croxton Smith awarded the first Challenge Certificates offered for the breed at Cruft's in 1926. In the years between 1926 and the present time the Afghan Hound has established himself firmly, if not very numerously, in both this country, the United States and Europe.

The Afghan of today may be more coiffeured and less shaggy than his ancestors, but in all essentials he remains unaltered—an active, athletic dog who bears himself with dignity and whose slanting, dark. eyes appear to gaze into distances beyond human ken. While an Afghan Hound may be polite to accredited friends in his master's house it is only to his own family that he gives his heart or shows his own distinct sense of humour.

DESCRIPTION OF THE AFGHAN HOUND

The longish coats, which extend to the feet of all four legs, the top-knot of long silky hair, the well-feathered ears (pendulous in shape), the smooth face and brow and the thin tail curving at the tip, are all striking features. The body is of the Greyhound type, but somewhat heavier and not so prominently arched at the loins. The brisket is deep, the belly tucked up, loins muscular. Neck arched, long and graceful, and well let into sloping shoulders. The tail is set low, giving a rounded appearance to the rump. Legs long, with hocks placed very low. Head long and with scarcely any stop. Eyes dark. Feet longish and well protected with hair. The usual colour is fawn, sometimes lightish, at others nearly red, and brindles are occasionally seen. Wherever they are seen they excite comment by their racial peculiarities and dignified bearing.

Basenjis

NEVER has a breed of dog attracted so much publicity as the first Basenjis to appear at British dog shows: not because of their beauty, their brains or their rarity, but simply because of their inability to bark! It was February, 1937, when a paragraph in the Press announced that barkless dogs would be on view at Cruft's. This resulted in extra police being called upon to control the crowds who wished to see these phenomena. In fact, although a Basenji may not bark, he does show pleasure or excitement by a sound that is best described as a kind of gurgling croon.

The dogs exhibited by Mrs Burn in 1937 were not the first of their breed to be brought from Africa to England—one had appeared at Cruft's in 1895 while in 1923 Lady Helen Nutting imported several from the Sudan. But these dogs from the jungles and deserts could not withstand the scourge of distemper and they all died. In the United States early attempts to introduce the breed met with the same difficulties and Basenjis were not established there until 1942.

In spite of the publicity of 1937 and the large number of people who had gazed at Mrs Burn's 'Bongo of Blean' at Cruft's that year, the war caused most people to forget all about Basenjis until 1945 when the newly-formed Basenjis Club held their first championship show in London. The winners there were the half-brother and sister 'Sunspot of the Congo' and 'Pilon Dulcinee', both of whom were descended from 'Bongo of Blean'.

The first champions in the breed were the brother and sister 'Ch. Brown Trout' and 'The Fern of the Congo', both owned by Miss Tudor Williams. 'Brown Trout' and 'Fern' were accidentally mated and produced a black and white son who became the great 'Ch. Black Magic of the Congo', who bore out the native superstition that black-marked dogs were lucky and should never be parted with.

The natives of the Sudan and the Congo use their dogs much as we use Spaniels—to hunt through scrub and undergrowth to turn out the game. Since it is difficult for the hunters to know the position of the dogs when they are working it is the custom to hang a bell or clapper made from a gourd about their necks. The natives value their dogs and are reluctant to part with them and it has not been easy to obtain fresh blood from the countries of their origin. Nevertheless, the breed is now popular in the United States and in Canada and importations have been made into America from the Congo; consequently it has been possible to mingle the best of American breeding with our own. The most notable example of this is probably 'Ch. Andersley Atlantic', who, on his dam's side, is a great grandson of 'Ch. Black Magic of the Congo', but, through his American sire, descends from stock imported from the Congo. 'Atlantic' himself has a litter sister, who is a champion here and another who has qualified in America, as well as having three American champion offspring.

One of the Basenji's most excellent characteristics is his great personal cleanliness; many of these dogs tongue wash themselves all over like a cat. Yet another good point is his moderate size. Some people may regard the Basenji's lack of normal voice as a disadvantage while to others it may appear as an advantage, but there is no doubt that the dog is quite capable of expressing his affection for his owner.

DESCRIPTION OF THE BASENJI

Well balanced and graceful, they have a slight waist and good heart room in the foreparts. The ears are carried erectly, their tails curl tightly, and their skin is peculiarly pliant. When the ears are pricked and they are excited, characteristic wrinkles appear on the forehead. Eyes small and dark hazel in colour. Their colour is chestnut with white points and tail tip, also black and white and black, tan and white. Cream-coloured Basenjis are heavily penalised. Average weight 22 to 24 lb. and height 16 to 17 in.

Basset Hounds

IN the early nineteen-fifties it appeared likely that Basset Hounds would become extinct in this country. For several years the breed had only been kept alive by the efforts of a tiny band of breeders which included Mrs Elms, perhaps more widely known for her Bloodhounds, and Miss Keevil who hunted a small pack around her home in Berkshire. It was the latter's importation from France of 'Grims Ulims de Barley' that gave the breed the fresh blood it so badly needed. It was in 1954 that there were signs of a revival of interest in the breed, when 63 Bassets were registered at the Kennel Club: in 1961 the total registrations were 552 and there is every sign that this figure will increase.

France and other parts of the Continent were undoubtedly the cradle of the Basset Hounds and there they were worked in small packs for both hunting game and for driving it towards the guns. It was probably the arrival of the sporting gun that gave sportsmen the idea that slow working, short legged hounds would be more useful to a man hunting on foot than the longer legged, fleeter hounds that were required when hunting was a mounted sport. Exactly what type of hounds were used in the development of the Basset history does not relate—several, one suspects, since several types of Basset emerged. Rough or smooth coats, straight legs, half crooked legs or crooked legs were acknowledged and acceptable types in France, but all of them had and have exquisitively sensitive noses and great independence. The voice of a Basset is deep and bell-like and a pack giving tongue is music indeed.

It was late in the nineteenth century before Basset Hounds first made their appearance in this country; the first being owned by Lord Galway and given to him by Comte Tournon de Montmelas. These soon passed into the possession of Lord Onslow. The earliest exhibitor of Basset Hounds was Sir Everett Millais, whose book *Bassets: Their Use and Breeding* is now extremely rare. His dog, 'Model', was the first dog of the breed to be exhibited and appeared at Wolverhampton Dog Show in 1875. 'Model' had been obtained from the great French authority on hounds, the Comte le Couteulx. Sir Everett admitted to not knowing of Lord Onslow's hounds and in consequence mating 'Model' to a Beagle bitch, but in 1877 the Beagle-bred stock was abandoned and a pure line established through 'Model's' daughter 'Garenne'.

In 1880 the Wolverhampton Show had classes for Bassets only and in 1883 the Basset Hound Club was formed. New breeders rallied round so rapidly that a hundred-and-twenty dogs of the breed appeared at a show held at the Aquarium in London in 1886. The leading breeders in those formative years were those already mentioned and Mr G. R. Krehl as well as Mrs C. C. Ellis. Mr Croxton Smith, who had been given a brace of hounds by Sir Everett Millais, bred through them 'Wantage' who sold for the then high price of £150. Queen Alexandra was a great lover of Basset Hounds and exhibited regularly. 'Sandringham Dido' was a winner at Cruft's in 1909 and royal exhibits continued to appear until 1921.

Modern attempts to alter the Basset and call them 'English Bassets' are to be deprecated and are not necessary as long as breeders of the true and accepted type continue to keep in mind that they are breeding hounds and not lap dogs.

DESCRIPTION OF THE BASSET HOUND

Hound markings either black-tan-and-white, lemon-and-white, flecked or pied. The body is long and powerful in proportion to the height. Strong loins, and great depth through the ribs. The deep brisket is said to be shaped like a man-of-war. The neck is thick and strong with considerable dewlap. The head, modelled as far as possible on that of the bloodhound, is a distinctive feature, betokening high breeding. It has a pronounced occiput or peak, and is long and narrow, of nearly equal width from peak to nose. The heavy flews meet squarely at the nose, and the brow and sides of the cheeks are profusely wrinkled. The long ears are placed low and when of the desirable fine texture they hang in graceful folds. The deep set eyes show the haw. The forelegs should fit closely to the chest; from the elbow to knee they incline inward, and then outwards to the large feet. They should be heavily boned. The stifles and hocks are well bent, and the thighs muscular. The stern, coarse underneath, is carried hound fashion. In the smooth variety, the coat is fine to the touch.

17

Beagles

ONE can hazard a guess that the term 'beagle' came into use late in the fifteenth century, for in 'Twelfth Night' Shakespeare made it an implied compliment to Maria, while James I used it as a term of affection for Robert Cecil, Earl of Salisbury who was his little 'beagill'. When the word was first applied to hounds is uncertain, although small hounds were undoubtedly known to the Normans and the Plantagenets. Queen Elizabeth I is said to have had beagles so small that one could be put into a lady's glove, but that was probably a flower of speech.

Beagles have enjoyed much royal favour—Dutch William owned a pack and so did George IV whose hounds often hunted on Brighton downs. But it must be understood that the Beagles of that period were not followed on foot but on horses and were, in fact, naught but small harriers. Sussex and the south-west have long been Beagle strongholds, but the custom of following these little hounds on foot seems to have arisen in the north of England.

The belief that a Beagle is a miniature or pygmy Foxhound is erroneous. A miniature hound maybe, but all through his long history the Beagle has retained attributes of character, outlook and shape of head that are entirely his own. The head characteristics are clearly seen in Philip Reinagle's charming illustration to the relevant chapter in *The Sportsman's Cabinet*.

There is nothing novel about Beagles appearing in the show ring. The first dog show to provide classes for the breed was at Birmingham in 1860, but for some now-forgotten reason no prizes were awarded. Not unnaturally there were many people who regretted seeing hounds at dog shows, but undoubtedly their appearance at such events did good, since it showed the wide differences of shape and make—not only in size and coats— but the variations in type between Beagles and the 'rabbit' or pocket Beagle. The formation of the Beagle Club in July, 1895, helped matters and a standard of points was drawn up that, excepting for the order of the paragraphs, is practically identical with the standard at the time of writing.

The United States has for many years been keenly interested in Beagles and for some time they were the most popular breed in that country. Most of their stock was originally imported from this country, but the passing of time and the rather different work expected of the American hounds have resulted in a variation of type that is very noticeable in the hounds imported to this country in the belief that fresh blood was needed here. The Beagle is also a great favourite in Canada, Australia and New Zealand.

Entered hounds, the property of various M.B., do not now appear at dog shows and this is not the place to enlarge on the pleasures of beagling or the virtues of various packs or the rights and wrongs of the schism between working and exhibition hounds.

The Beagle has so much charm of character and appearance that it is easy to understand why he has left the pack for the parlour in steadily increasing numbers. At Cruft's in 1948 only ten Beagles were exhibited, whereas in 1961 there were 116— registrations have risen from 154 in 1954 to 2,047 seven years later. One hopes, however, that breeders and owners of Beagles will not be so dazzled by popularity that they will lose sight of the purpose for which their hounds have been bred for well over five hundred years.

DESCRIPTION OF THE BEAGLE

The head, which is of fair length, is powerful without being coarse; skull domed, moderately wide, with an indication of peak; stop well defined, muzzle not snipy and flews pronounced. Eyes brown, dark hazel or hazel. Ears long, set on low, fine in texture, and hanging in a graceful fold close to the cheek. Neck moderately long and slightly arched. Throat shows some dewlap. Shoulders clean and slightly sloping. Body short between the couplings, well let down in chest; ribs fairly well sprung and well ribbed up, with powerful and not tucked-up loins. Thighs very muscular; stifles and hocks well bent and hocks well let down. Forelegs quite straight, having substance, and round in bone. Feet round, well knuckled-up, and strongly padded. Stern of moderate length set on high and carried gaily, but not curled over the back. Any recognised hound colour is approved. They may have either smooth or rough coats, but the smooth are much the more general.

Bloodhounds

THE last years of the sixteenth century were important in the history and development of the Bloodhound. It was in 1577 that Hollingshead tells us: 'There is a law also amongst the Borderers in time of peace, that who so denieth entrance or sute of a Sleuth hound in pursuit made after fellons and stolend goods, shal be holden as accessorie unto a theft'. Hector Boece, as well as Hollingshead and other writers, refers to this hunting of felons on the Scottish Borders by hounds variously referred to as 'sleuth', 'slot' or 'bloodhounds'.

There is no absolute proof, but there are reasonable grounds for assuming that these tracking hounds descended from the 'Black' hounds kept by St Hubert in the eighth century and whose strain lived on in the monastery that bears his name in the Ardennes. These 'Black' hounds are described as being generally 'black running into tan with tan markings over the eyes, and feet the same colour: long ears'. William the Conqueror and his followers were responsible for bringing these hounds to England and others were brought over on various later occasions and Henry IV of France presented 'a team' to James I of England. Hounds of this type were generally used as *limiers*, *limers* or *lemors*, a term derived from lyame, a leash. A *limier* was chosen from the rest of the pack for the keenness of his scent and staunchness on a line; it was his job to work leashed and to find and move a stag, when the rest of the pack took over. The harbourer and the *limier* kept as close to the hunt as possible, taking care not to cross the line; if, however, the stag ran into company or the pack checked, the *limier* was called up to put them right again.

It is easy to understand that the instincts of such a hound could easily be diverted to working on human scent and references to the use of hounds for the tracking of criminals can be found in writings of both the sixteenth and seventeenth centuries and the instinct is now deeply rooted in the Bloodhound. Hounds exported from this country were used in the Americas and Africa for the tracking of runaway slaves, but since the true Bloodhound has little or no wish to attack his quarry when he has found him, hounds used for this grim purpose were usually crossed with larger or more savage breeds.

Breeders of Bloodhounds have wisely kept the instincts of their hounds alive and although it is seldom that they are now used for hunting criminals, tracking meetings are frequently held in various parts of the New Forest. Some hounds run mute and give tongue with a deep, musical note only when their objective is in sight while others give tongue the whole time they are working.

One of the most successful of the early hounds to appear at a dog show was 'Druid' owned by Mr Grantly Berkeley, while in the final years of the last century and the opening years of this Mr. Edwin Brough owned many outstanding hounds and he, himself, considered the brothers 'Burgundy' and 'Bardolph' the best he had ever bred.

At the present time Bloodhounds are not the most usual dogs to see around, nevertheless the demand is in excess of the supply, for those who have once given their hearts to a Bloodhound will never subsequently place it elsewhere.

DESCRIPTION OF THE BLOODHOUND

It will be seen that the head is very long and narrow; this formation gives greater room for the olfactory faculties. The head should be covered with a mass of loose skin falling in wrinkles, and the long, silky ears are set on low. The eyes are not bloodshot, but the peculiar appearance is caused by the lower lids being dragged down by the flews under the inner skin or haw. The Bloodhound's back is somewhat longer than that of the Foxhound, but there should be no weakness of the loins. Legs straight, with heavy bone, and feet rounded. The usual colour is black-and-tan, but there are also reds or red-and-tan. The hound should be well up on its feet, should move freely, and should have a general appearance of great nobility and dignity. In disposition they are Nature's gentlemen, it being unusual to meet a bad-tempered or sulky hound.

Borzois

T HE Borzois or Russian Wolfhounds were a product of Imperial Russia—nowhere
except in a land of such vast plains and forests or under such a social regime would
it have been possible to breed and keep these lovely hounds in such great numbers;
to hunt them with such flamboyance or with such a total disregard of money or time.

The origins of the Borzois are uncertain although in thirteenth-century Russian
writings there are some references to the coursing of hares and, somewhat later, Peter
Michailovich Gubinin wrote a treatise on Russian hunting and describes seven types of
Russian hunting dog. These large packs of hounds were owned and their strains jealously
guarded by various noble families and it is clear that with such tremendous distances
involved any inter-breeding of the various packs was impossible even if it had been
desired.

The year 1861 brought about a big upheaval in Russia, for it was then that serfdom
nominally came to an end and many of the big estates were broken up and, for a time,
the keeping of such enormous numbers of hounds ceased. However, after not more than
a decade many of the estates were re-established. With the formation in 1873 of the
Imperial Association for the Propagation of Hounds and the Regulation of Hunting the
quality of the hounds became a little more important than the quantity.

The Perchino kennels, owned by the Grand Duke Nikolai Nikolavich, were a model of
their kind and housed two packs of English Foxhounds each of twenty-five couple, fifteen
English Greyhounds as well as a hundred-and-fifty Borzois. Since hunting could not always
take place within reach of the kennels it was quite usual for hounds, horses, guests,
staff, carts, carriages and kitchens to be loaded on special trains and conveyed from
hunting ground to hunting ground, such expeditions lasting for weeks at a time.

When hunting wolves, for Borzois were only occasionally used on any other type of
game, the hounds usually hunted in pairs for the dog would go for the throat of the wolf
while the bitch attacked the flank. The wolves were driven from the cover of the woods
by the Foxhounds and kept on a straight course by beaters. The Borzois were not expected
to kill—indeed it was a fault if they did, except in self defence—but to course and pull
down and hold their quarry until the mounted huntsman arrived either to despatch or
muzzle and strap the wolf. The Revolution brought about the dissolution of all the great
kennels, and as far as one can tell, the disappearance of the hounds.

It is nearly a hundred years since Borzois attracted attention in this country and the
first notable hounds were a pair presented by the Czar to Queen Victoria. Princess
Alexandra was greatly attracted to the breed and soon became an exhibitor. The
acclimatising of the hounds seems to have presented difficulties in the early days, but
fifty hounds, including twenty from famous Russian kennels, were exhibited in London
in 1890. The visitors were subsequently put up for sale and 'Oudar' and 'Laska' fetched
£200 each. 'Oudar' was bought by the Duchess of Newcastle as a foundation for her
subsequently famous 'of Notts' kennel.

Borzoi breeders in this country have faced and surmounted the difficulties of keeping
such big dogs throughout two world wars, but although these hounds are not the most
familiar of the hound breeds they are certainly the most lovely.

DESCRIPTION OF THE BORZOI

Built on the lines of the Greyhound, they are bigger and more powerful all through, and their formation should indicate speed, strength and symmetry. The appearance is greatly enhanced by the long silky coat, which is either flat, wavy or rather curly. Colours are usually white or white with fawn, brindle, red, blue or grey markings. The head is extraordinarily long and lean, with a flat and narrow skull, and in profile it appears somewhat Roman nosed. Ears small and thin, and placed far back on the head. Chest very deep and somewhat narrow; back much arched and rather bony. Powerful loins with well-developed muscles; thighs long, and good second thighs. Stifles slightly bent and hocks set fairly low. Front legs straight with flat bone. Strong pasterns and feet rather long. The well-feathered tail is not carried gaily. The height of the dog should be 29 in. upwards at the shoulders. They display an air of great distinction.

23

Dachshunds

ALTHOUGH classified as hounds there are very few Dachshunds who now work as such. Even though many members of the family have good noses, the work they were intended for—badger drawing—requires the characteristics of a terrier rather than those of a hound. It is, however, as companions that Dachshunds, whether large or small, smooth, rough or long coated, have achieved popularity.

The smooth-coated Dachshund is the original type, but opinions differ as to its antiquity. It has been suggested that an Egyptian drawing of the eleventh dynasty (about 2100 B.C.) of a long bodied, short legged bitch with a pointed, fox-like head represents an early Dachshund, but there has always been some controversy over this. However, Dr Max Hilzeimer, a well-known authority, believed that Dachshunds were entirely German in origin, since remains of dogs of the type had been excavated in several Romano-Germanic settlements.

That Dachshunds, roughly in the shape and form that we know them today, have long been used in Germany both for badger and rabbit digging as well as for companions is certain but much has been done here to advance the breed. It is notable that the English Dachshund Club was founded some seven years before the German Teckel Club.

It was in 1870 that a dog described as a 'German Badger Hound' appeared in an English dog show, and in 1873 three 'German Daxhounds' were exhibited at Birmingham while five appeared at a show held at the Crystal Palace later that year. Two of these, 'Xaverl' and 'Waldine', eventually produced 'Hans', 'Centa', 'Zarrah' and 'Zaidee', all of whom became notable.

About 1900 English-bred Dachshunds tended to become too large and too coarse and a German judge horrified exhibitors by proclaiming that the dogs brought before him were not even recognisable as Dachshunds! In consequence several dogs were imported from Germany and from 'Brandesburton Filius' descended 'Ch. Honeystone' founder of a famous line and probably the best dog to have been bred in this country up to that time.

During the First World War it became a foolish fashion to revile Dachshunds, but by about 1920 opinion had swung round and the breed were again in great demand and two importations—'Remigan Max' and 'Ch. Faust v. d. Furstenburg'—brought in fresh blood. It was at this period that British breeders realised that there were other types of Dachshund—wire-haired and long coated—the former probably produced by a Dandie Dinmont Terrier cross and the latter by the use of a spaniel. Although the first long coated Dachshund had been seen in this country about 1908 it was a number of years before this variety aroused much interest and it was not recognised by the Kennel Club until 1931.

There are now miniature varieties of all three types of Dachshund and in their case eleven pounds is the top weight acceptable and, other points being equal, the smaller they are the better.

There is no breed of dog more loyal and affectionate nor with a more determined character than a Dachshund and his stratagems for gaining personal advantage are evidence of his intelligence; it is, therefore, essential that a dog of this breed should have firm discipline if he is not to become the master of his owner.

DESCRIPTION OF THE DACHSHUND

Smart, active and sound. The forelegs are very short, and strong in bone, elbows fit close to the ribs. The upper arm is at right-angles to the shoulder blade and the lower arm is inclined slightly inwards, making the crook. Forefeet large, round and strong. Hocks are well bent, and the hind feet are smaller in bone and narrower than the front. Chest deep and oval. The long narrow head tapers to the point of the muzzle; the stop is not pronounced; skull slightly arched in profile. Ears broad, of moderate length, and well rounded. Eyes of medium size, oval, set obliquely, and dark, except in chocolates and dapples Body long and muscular, the line of the back being slightly depressed at shoulders and slightly arched over loins. *Standard (smooth-haired).* Weight up to 25 lb. Coat short, dense and smooth. *Miniature (smooth-haired).* Weight must not exceed 11 lb. *Standard (long-haired).* Coat soft, straight or slightly waved resembling that of an Irish Setter. *Miniature (long-haired).* Weight must not exceed 11 lb. *Standard (wire-haired).* Coat short, harsh and even with an undercoat. Bushy eyebrows. Beard on chin. *Miniature (wire-haired).* Weight must not exceed 12 lb.

Deerhounds

SINCE ownership of Deerhounds was the prerogative of the early Scottish kings and their nobles these hounds were carefully bred and highly valued early in Scotland's history. Stories of the breed's sagacity and hunting prowess occur constantly in the works of the early Scottish historians. Nevertheless, the origin of the breed is obscure although there is undoubtedly a degree of kinship with the Greyhound. It is probably due to the Phoenician traders who visited these islands that we are indebted for the earliest hounds of this type.

A rough, harsh and weather-resisting coat was a necessity for a hound who had to work in the mountainous Scottish country, and who had to be both swift and strong to hunt, hold and bring down a stag over such rough and wild terrain. The earliest pictorial representations of Scottish hounds are carved on stones believed to date from 800 A.D. Understandably, these give but a vague indication of the appearance of the dogs, but by comparison with the accompanying figures of horses and their riders it is plain that they were both large and powerful and that they did, in fact, seize the deer either by the haunch or the throat.

Hector Boece (1465-1536), the Scottish historian, recounts several incidents in which Deerhounds feature and tells how Robert Bruce granted Sir William St Clair the Forest of Pentland Firth in 'free forestrie' when the latter's hounds 'Help' and 'Hold' had won the wager in which their master's head was forfeit had they lost. Sir William lies in Rosslyn Chapel, his hound at his feet, while his descendants still owned notable hounds many generations later.

By the sixteenth century the *tainchell* or deer drive was a favourite amusement and there remains a famous account of the vast *tainchell* organised by the Earl of Atholl for the entertainment of Mary, Queen of Scots. Two thousand highlanders drove all the deer from 'the woods and hills of Athole, Badenach, Mar, Moray and all the counties round about' to make a royal holiday.

By the latter years of the eighteenth century improved firearms and the increase of cultivated lands brought the true Deerhound to hard times, since all that was required by sportsmen was some kind of a dog capable of tracking down a wounded deer. In the years that immediately followed the publication of *Days of Deerstalking* (1838), for which Archibald M'Neill of Colonsay wrote the final chapter and drew attention to the great dearth of pure-bred hounds, the 'Colonsay Revival' gathered impetus. The efforts of Lord Colonsay, Mr Horatio Ross of Rossie and Mr Donald Robertson of Mull, as well as of several English sportsmen, brought about the revival of genuine deer-coursing, then almost obsolete, and the production of pure-bred hounds for the purpose. 'No gun', wrote Lord Colonsay when describing his object and eventual success, 'was ever taken to the hill—the whole done by the dogs'. Another who was much interested in the revival and the hounds was Sir Walter Scott, owner of the famous 'Maida', who, nevertheless, was not quite pure bred.

At Birmingham in 1860 the first recorded all-breed dog show was held and Colonel Inge's 'Valiant' and 'Brimstone' appeared and won, and the breed appeared regularly at dog shows in the years that followed. Wise, faithful and dignified the Deerhound of today remains as a living heritage from the past.

DESCRIPTION OF THE DEERHOUND

A tall, rough-coated dog. Dogs average 30 to 32 in., bitches 28 to 30 in. at shoulder. Colours wheaten, brindle, grey, the last being the most popular. White is a blemish save for a blaze on the chest or a tip to the tail, which should be carried low without curl. Shoulders well laid back, great depth of brisket and well-sprung ribs. A characteristic is width and strength across the loins, which should be well arched. Stifles well bent and hocks low to ground. The head is carried high on a long, strong neck with prominent nape. The clean-cut skull, flat, with the ears set high, is coated with softer, longer hair than the body, and plenty of shaggy eyebrow. The muzzle strong, teeth and lips level. Eyes dark, deep set, full of expression. This wistful, far-away expression is the keynote of the character of the breed.

Elkhounds

T HE Elkhound is very typical of several breeds of Scandinavian hunting dog. It is obvious from his stocky, almost heavy, build that he is not intended for a running hound; he is capable of great endurance but not high speed.

In Scandinavia elk hunting takes place late in the autumn in districts where there are large tracts of forest. At the present time elk are carefully preserved and the number of beasts to be killed during a season is strictly regulated. In consequence, the earlier habit of driving the beasts in droves towards a line of waiting guns has been discontinued. When these battues were popular it was the Elkhounds' work to track down all the injured beasts so that they could be put out of their misery. At the present time it is more usual for two or perhaps four hounds to work ahead of their human companions seeking the scent of elk. The dogs must work hard and over a wide area, but not so fast that they outpace their masters. The scent once found, the dogs follow it up, still in silence. But once the elk is in sight they bark intermittently to keep the followers in touch with their position. Moving quietly, the dogs circle the elk; two well-trained dogs can thus keep the beast within a narrow area for half an hour or more and the hunters can get close enough to be certain of shooting to kill. Once the beast has fallen the dogs rush in and are allowed to tear the flesh and lap the blood.

Excavations in old 'kitchen middens', the rubbish heaps of the old Danish and Norse settlements, have brought to light bones and skulls that show that the hounds of today must have been very similar to those of the distant past and probably did much the same work in much the same way.

Elkhounds first came to this country in 1876. 'Blue' and 'Jager' appeared in classes for foreign dogs at various shows, but the breed did not arouse much interest and by 1915 it had practically died out with the notable exception of a dog named 'Woden' who was born in the early years of the First World War. After the war there was a widespread interest in all matters canine, including Elkhounds, and a number were imported, while 'Ch. Woden', as he became, greatly assisted in the revival of the breed. In 1923 the British Elkhound Society was founded with Lady Dorothy Wood (later Viscountess Halifax) as its president. Lady Halifax and Lieut. Colonel Scovell imported 'Binna' and 'Bob av Glitre', while two other important animals were the future champions 'Finnegutten' and 'Gaupa av Glitre'—the latter bitch has a most important place in both British and American breed history.

The controversy over type—since the hounds of Norway varied somewhat from those of Sweden—has now abated and Elkhounds of the highest quality are bred in this country.

Despite his heavy coat the Elkhound needs the minimum of grooming to keep him clean and healthy, while his constitution is sound and hardy. The very nature of his work has ensured that an Elkhound has an independence of character and outlook and it is unlikely that he will be as unquestioning in his obedience as a gun dog or an Alsatian. Nevertheless, when well trained he makes a good guard and an intelligent and faithful companion.

DESCRIPTION OF THE ELKHOUND

In appearance it is a handsome, virile, sporting dog of compact, medium build, erect, pointed ears, a tightly-curled tail and heavy weather-resisting coat. He is not long in the back, but must be muscular, elastic and sinuous in movement, with a deep chest, well-sprung ribs, strong neck, and sturdy limbs. He has to be capable of feats of great endurance when used in Norway in hunting the elk. The colour is attractive, being grey with black ends to the longer outer hairs. On back and haunches the surface tips of the long hair are usually darker than at the roots, and the ears may be black. The chest, under parts and legs are light inclining to silver-white. Pronounced dark markings below the knees are regarded as a blemish. A dark eye is preferred with a forward outlook; the oblique position, giving a wolfish expression, is undesirable.

29

Finnish Spitz

T HE Finnish Spitz, sometimes known as the 'Finnish Cock-eared Dogs' but often more affectionately referred to by their admirers as 'Finkies', made their earliest appearances in this country during 1927 and 1928. Commander Sir Edward Chichester fell in love with the breed while in Finland and imported a brace which were exhibited at several of the leading dog shows. Their very charming appearance and lively ways attracted a good deal of attention. Before long other importations were made and the first English-bred litter opened their eyes in a new land.

The early history of the Finnish Spitz has not been explored in any great detail, but it is certain that dogs of the type have been known in their native country for a very long period and that they are collateral relations of several other native Scandinavian breeds. It is believed that dogs of the type were introduced by early tribes migrating from the east northwards. Without doubt this type of Spitz dog has been known and used in Finland for several hundred years and while primarily valued as a hunting dog it had a good secondary use since the breed make excellent watchdogs.

It is as hunters of game birds that 'Finkies' are mainly worked in their own country although they can be trained to track animals as far apart in size as elks and squirrels. When working on birds such as the capercailzie they track them over the snow or through the forests and when the bird rises and perches on a tree the dog marks the spot, giving tongue both loud and long, until the guns arrive. A skilful dog is highly valued and a form of Field Trial is often held to assess the ability of the dogs.

Earlier in the present century it was hard to find a pure-bred and really typical Finnish Spitz in its native country, partly owing to lack of interest in selective breeding and partly because many dogs had been crossed with other Scandinavian breeds whose work was somewhat the same. It was not until the Finnish Kennel Club began to take an interest in its native breeds that careful breeding received any encouragement. The pair of 'Finkies' imported by Sir Edward Chichester were of excellent type and of a particularly good, rich red colour.

The Finnish Spitz breed achieved championship status in 1935 and the first dogs to get their title were 'Siro of Boydon', 'Andy of Tulchan' and the bitch 'Hammon Ary of Tulchan', owned respectively by Miss R. Parker, Miss Lurcock and Lady Kitty Ritson. That admirers of the 'Finkie' are faithful to the breed is proved by the fact that some of the people who were breeding and exhibiting in 1935 are still doing so at the present time. Nevertheless, the breed has never achieved tremendous popularity despite its charming appearance, moderate size and high degree of intelligence: this can probably be accounted for by the fact that the breed's most outstanding characteristic is its great activity of both mind and body. In consequence a 'Finkie' needs to spend its life where it can be constantly 'on the go', yet untrammelled freedom has its dangers for a dog whose deeply-rooted instincts urge him to pursue any feathered creature that may cross his path. Where, however, these dogs can live in the right conditions they make gay, faithful and charming companions.

DESCRIPTION OF THE FINNISH SPITZ

They are sometimes called cock-eared dogs. The Finnish standard describes the head as of medium size with forehead somewhat arched. Muzzle narrow and tapering evenly. Ears mobile, erect and pointed. Eyes of medium size, lively, full of expression and preferably dark. Back straight and strong. Chest deep. Slightly drawn up at belly. Shoulders comparatively upright. Forelegs firm and straight. Hind legs strong and comparatively straight at hocks. Feet preferably round. Tail curled and pressing on the thigh. Coat on head and front of legs short, longish on body and semi-erect or erect. Stiffer on neck and back. Longer and coarser on shoulders. Feathered on thighs and tail. Soft undercoat. Colour brownish red or yellowish brown on back. Lighter inside ears on cheeks and underparts. White permissible on chest and feet. Height at withers and length of body in males $17\frac{1}{2}$ in., 20 in.; in bitches $15\frac{1}{2}$ in., 18 in.

31

Greyhounds

SWIFT hounds who hunted primarily by sight have a well recorded history stretching over some four thousand years. There is scarcely a writer on sport, from Xenophon to the present day, who has not had something to say about the hounds who later became known as Greyhounds.

The origin of the name Greyhound or *grehound* has never been satisfactorily explained but it certainly does not derive from the colour since we know that these hounds have always been as varied in colour as their owners' preferences. Grattius, writing in the last century B.C., said 'Choose the greyhound pied with black and white: he runs more swift than thought or winged light', but Oppian, writing later, considered that black and white hounds were over sensitive to temperature. Edward, second Duke of York, author of *The Mayster of Game* (c. 1406) remarks 'the best hue is rede falow, with a black moselle'.

The Greyhound has always been bred for hunting and built for speed and endurance. That it has not altered in any essential points from classical times to the present day is proved by the numerous representations that appear in classical art—sometimes as a companion of Artemis or Diana in her role of goddess of hunting. That both Greeks and Egyptians used their hounds for coursing is certain and that such coursing was regarded as a sport rather than a means of filling the larder is proved by the words of Arrian: 'Whosoever course hares with hounds should neither loose them near the hare, nor more than a pair at a time'.

Whether Greyhounds are the oldest of the gazehounds (hounds who hunt mainly by sight) is a moot point, but they are undoubtedly closely related to the ancient hounds from further east and are kin of the deerhounds and wolfhounds of these islands, as well as later arrivals such as Italian Greyhounds, Borzois and Whippets.

Queen Elizabeth I is believed to have instructed the Duke of Norfolk to lay down a code of rules for coursing and that knowledgeable man, William Shakespeare, certainly knew something of the sport when he wrote: 'How doth your fallow greyhound, sir? I hear he was outrun on Cotele' or the more familiar 'I see you stand like greyhounds in the slips straining upon the start . . .'.

It was the eccentric Lord Orford who laid the foundations of coursing as it is known today when he established the Swaffham Coursing Society in 1776. Lord Orford owned 'Czarina', winner of 47 matches, and it was to see her run that her owner rose from his sick bed but fell dead as she won. 'Czarina' was the grand-dam of Colonel Topham's famous black dog 'Snowball' who, with his brother and sister Major and Sylvia, became the ancestors of so many good hounds. In 1836 the Waterloo Cup was first run and, later, won three times by 'Master M'Grath'. The National Coursing Club came into existence in 1858. At Hendon in 1876 Greyhounds chased a mechanical hare in public for the first time but it was some fifty years later that track racing became popular.

The Greyhound is not, as so many imagine, lacking in intelligence and makes an excellent house dog and companion provided his natural instinct is checked from his earliest days and he is never allowed to chase small living creatures that he may see at large.

DESCRIPTION OF THE GREYHOUND

The Greyhound is a strongly-built, upstanding dog of generous proportions, muscular with symmetrical formation; long head and neck, deep chest, sound legs and feet, and possessed of great stamina and endurance. The skull is flat with slight stop, powerful jaws, and bright intelligent eyes, dark in colour. The ears are small of fine texture. Neck is long and muscular and well let into the shoulder. The forelegs are long and straight. Feet of moderate length, with compact, well-knuckled toes and strong pads. The tail is long, set on rather low, strong at the root and tapering to the point, carried low and slightly curved. The coat is fine and close and the colours are black, white, red, blue, fawn, fallow, brindle, or any of these colours broken with white. The ideal height for dogs is between 28 and 30 in., and for bitches 27 and 28 in.

Irish Wolfhounds

IN the myths and legends that make up the early story of Ireland we catch the first glimpses of the huge hounds who were the forerunners of the Wolfhounds, to whom so many references are made in Ireland's later history. It is not possible to date with any accuracy many of these early references, but the story of the famous hero Cu-Chulainn—Cu means a hound—has a certain interest. Cu-Chulainn got his name from an incident in his boyhood when the great hound of Chulainn the smith set on him. In the struggle the boy killed him. Overcome with remorse at his deed, he undertook to remain and guard the smith for one year while he trained a whelp of the old hound's to carry on the duty. Since all the legends stress Cu-Chulainn's fidelity to his word, he carried out his penance; but throughout the rest of his life he was always accompanied by a pack of hounds and often took them to Scotland for the hunting. Here we see the possible earliest link between the Wolfhound of Ireland and the Deerhound of Scotland who, to this day, bear considerable resemblance to each other.

Although Rome never raised her standards in Ireland, Quintus Aurelius Symmachus wrote from Rome (c. A.D. 393) to his brother Flavianus then in Britain thanking him for his gift of seven hounds, 'at which Rome was astonished'.

All the Irish kings prized their hounds and many tales of their courage and fidelity can be read in *The Book of Leinster* (twelfth century).

Depictions of these early hounds are uncommon, but from those that do exist it is clear that they were, in fact, of large size but often of variegated colours—light splashed with darker markings.

During the sixteenth, seventeenth and eighteenth centuries these Irish hounds were in great demand as presents for foreign rulers and notabilities, but subsequent to 1652 Oliver Cromwell made it illegal to export Wolfhounds owing to their increasing rarity and the damage done by wolves. Nevertheless, there are many records which show that this decree must have been evaded and that many a brace of hounds joined some royal kennel.

It was, however, when the wolves had become all but extinct in Ireland that the Wolfhounds fell on evil days and there are many references to individual hounds as 'the last of their race' or to crosses with the Great Dane. By the middle of the nineteenth century the pure breed appeared to be extinct.

About 1859 Captain George Graham, who had previously been interested in Scottish Deerhounds, decided to make the revival of the Irish Wolfhound his great interest, and until his death in 1907—when it is said he had spent £20,000 on his hobby—he remained the chief promoter of the breed. Although Captain Graham subsequently obtained a number of hounds of varying degrees of purity, his first was 'Faust', a powerful red dog bred by the Rev. Lane Fox; this dog was only $29\frac{1}{2}$ in. at the shoulder, but this dog's great-grandson, who admittedly had Deerhound blood, reached the height of $32\frac{3}{4}$ in.; so size was fairly quickly regained, although soundness was more elusive. Another breeder who did much to re-establish the breed was Mr Everett, whose 'Felixstowe' prefix was to achieve great fame in the years to follow.

At the present time the Irish Wolfhound is as noble in appearance and character as his distant ancestors—slow to anger and quick to defend; faithful and loyal to his last breath.

DESCRIPTION OF THE IRISH WOLFHOUND

The tallest dog in the world, reaching as much as $37\frac{3}{4}$ in., it will be seen that the Irish Wolfhound has the shape of a massive Greyhound, with a rough, hard coat. The recognised colours are grey, brindle, red, fawn, black or pure white, but the last two are seldom seen. They carry great bone and a lot of muscle, with long second thighs and hocks well let down. The chest is very deep and wide and the back rather long, with arched loins. The well-arched neck is also rather long, and very strong and muscular without any loose skin at the throat. The head is long with a skull that is neither too heavy nor too light. They can gallop fast enough to catch a wolf, and they are able to course hares, though they are not so clever at killing as the Greyhound.

Rhodesian Ridgebacks

ALTHOUGH something of a parvenu the Rhodesian Ridgeback is steadily becoming more widely appreciated in this country and no dog makes a wiser companion or a more respected guard. He is, however, large and powerful and if he is to give of his best he needs space and discipline.

It is the ridge of hair along the spine lying in the reverse direction to the normal that gives the breed its name and is its outstanding physical characteristic. Inherited from the Hottentot dogs, who got it from no one knows where, this ridge has aroused much controversy.

The story of the Ridgebacks began in South Africa where the Boer farmers required powerful dogs of great courage and strong physique, which were also resistant to ticks and thirst, to guard their homes and accompany them on hunting expeditions. The material they had to work with was a motley pack of tykes, many of them the descendants of the dogs that had accompanied the early Dutch, German and Huguenot settlers, plus a sprinkling of the old slave traders' Bloodhounds and Mastiffs. Many of these were mated to the shaggy, ugly Hottentot dogs who much resembled jackals except for the fact that the hair on their backs lay in a peculiar manner. Their antecedants were of less interest than the fact that they were tough, courageous and not without intelligence.

Nothing much might have been heard of these Boer dogs if in 1887 a Boer farmer had not given two to the Rev. Charles Helm who took them to Bulawayo where they were borrowed by the well-known big game hunter, Cornelius van Rooyen. Although impressed by their hunting ability and courage van Rooyen considered these dogs too big and heavy and lacking in scenting ability for his purpose. To improve matters various crosses were tried of which those with Collies and Airedales seem to have been the most successful. The ridge remained a dominant characteristic and became a hall mark of a type of dog which found much favour with the white settlers and big game hunters.

In 1922 the Rhodesian Ridgeback (Lion Dog) Club was formed and about thirty dogs, all with the ridge but otherwise a rather assorted collection, were presented at a meeting of the young club and their good and bad features weighed up and discussed. From this meeting a standard of points was formulated which is, in the main, similar to that accepted at the present time.

In 1929 Mrs Foljambe brought two Ridgebacks to England and their peculiarity, plus the belief that these dogs were expected to track and pull down a lion by their own efforts, aroused a great deal of interest, but the ordinary citizen, not having any lions around, was apt to feel that such a dog might be wasted on him and possibly be a danger to others. Since then it has been explained that these dogs are not intended to be single-handed lion killers, but their purpose is to harry lions and other game from cover and bring them to bay so that their master can approach and shoot.

The last war limited any increase in the numbers of dogs bred in this country, but after 1945 further importations were made and 'Justa of Banda', one of the two Ridgebacks presented to Queen Elizabeth II, proved to be a very useful and dominant sire who did much for the breed in this country. In 1954 there were a sufficient number of dogs registered at the Kennel Club for the breed to be granted championship status and 'Maiduba of Manscross', a son of 'Justa of Banda' became the breed's first champion.

DESCRIPTION OF THE RHODESIAN RIDGEBACK

The peculiarity of this breed is the ridge on the back, which is formed by hair growing in the opposite direction to the rest of the coat. The ridge of hair must be clearly defined, tapering towards the stern; there should be two identical crowns or flourishes across the withers. This ridge of hair is the escutcheon of the breed, without it a dog is not recognised as belonging to the breed. The Ridgeback is a muscular and active dog. A mature dog should stand 25 to 27 in. in height and be about 80 lb. in weight. The coat is short, dense, sleek and glossy, the colour light wheaten to red wheaten, and a little white on the chest and toes is permissible.

37

Salukis

THE Saluki and the Afghan Hound are undoubtedly related and both of them, together with the Greyhound, are true gazehounds, hunting almost entirely by sight and placing a minimum of reliance on their powers of scent. Whether the Saluki or the Afghan is the older breed is a problem that will probably never be satisfactorily settled. The Afghan Hounds may have been in the Ark when it ran aground on Ararat, but the Salukis accompanied the Pharoahs on their hunting expeditions and worked for them in much the same way as they still work for their Arab masters. Depictions of hounds strongly resembling Salukis have frequently been found in Egyptian tombs and one of the most interesting came from the tomb of Rechmara (1400 B.C.).

It is, however, to the Arab tribes that we are mainly indebted for the Saluki as we know him today. Salukis are widely scattered over Persia and the Near East, but wherever they are found there has been contact with the Arabs at no far distant date. As a Mohammedan the Arab scorns all dogs, but has an undying love for his Saluki who, he says, is not a dog but a hound: with him he will share his food and his tent. The origin of the word Saluki is said to be 'Saluk', a now vanished Arabian town once notable for the excellence of its hounds.

Desert hares and gazelle are the Saluki's natural quarry and these are sometimes hunted with the aid of a falcon, but the best and most valued hounds hunted alone or in pairs. Possibly not as fast as a Greyhound but with greater endurance, a Saluki would hunt a gazelle for three or four miles and pull it down at the end. However highly valued the Saluki, he seldom led a life of luxury or ease—if his master's supply of food was short so was his, and for the same reason that a hungry man draws his belt tight, so many a Saluki wore a strap around his loins.

To the Hon. Florence Amherst goes the credit of being the first person to put the Saluki before the British dog loving public. As the daughter of the celebrated archaeologist, Lord Amherst of Hackney, Miss Amherst knew the breed well in its native country. Her first two importations were two puppies bred by the sheiks of a Bedouin tribe and other hounds followed—from Syria, Arabia, Persia and Mesopotamia. It was not easy to get hounds of pure breeding, for the sheiks were reluctant to part with good stock. It was not until after the First World War that the breed made real progress. Brigadier Lance had brought two hounds home with him and others followed. 'Sarona-Sarona' and the black-and-tan dog who became 'Ch. Sarona Kelb' made a tremendous impression and the last named was an extremely dominant sire who did the breed a great deal of good.

Hardly were the Salukis well established with a club, enthusiastic breeders, and good entries at shows, when World War II put an end to progress. Although breeding and showing started again as soon as it was possible, things have never been quite so bright again. Registrations are fairly steady and good dogs appear in the show ring, but the breed does not appear to be progressing as fast as it should considering its graceful appearance and moderate size.

The character of the Saluki is dignified—somewhat aloof with strangers but affectionate and faithful to his owner and family. Seldom aggressive with his own kind and possessing a sound constitution, the Saluki has many virtues and few vices.

DESCRIPTION OF THE SALUKI

The height of a dog may vary from 23 to 28 in., bitches usually being much smaller. The head is long and narrow, skull moderately wide between ears and not domed. The long, drooping ears are covered with long, silky hair, and the legs and tail are feathered. The rest of the coat is smooth, and of a soft, silky texture. Eyes dark to hazel; neck long and supple; chest deep and moderately narrow; shoulders sloping and set well back; forelegs straight with great length from elbow to knee. The feet are not cat-shape but are moderately long and very strong. The long tail is carried in a curve. Colours are white, cream, fawn, golden, red, grizzle-and-tan, black-and-tan, or tricolour. The smooth variety is identical except that it is not feathered.

Whippets

WHIPPETS, as a breed, came quietly into existence during the nineteenth century under the auspices of the sporting miners of the north of England. These men wanted a dog, smaller than a Greyhound, who would course rabbits in a limited or enclosed space. Having achieved a dog suitable for their purpose, by means that have never been clearly documented, these North Country sportsmen evolved another sport that gave their dogs an opportunity of using their unquestionable speed and power in competitive events. This amusement came to be known as 'rag racing'. It was inexpensive and easy to organise since it required only a small amount of space, dogs with a good turn of speed over short distances, as well as some skill on the part of the dogs' handlers or owners. That it offered opportunity for betting was a further attraction. One of this amusements greatest virtues, however, was that it superseded the cruel so-called sport of rabbit coursing where the rabbit, turned loose in a small, enclosed area, had little chance of escape.

The foundation breeds on which the Whippet came into existence were undoubtedly the Greyhound and the Italian Greyhound, the smallest of the former breed being mated to the largest of the latter. Italian Greyhounds—those miniature replicas of the Greyhound—had been favourites of royal and noble families for hundreds of years and there was nothing against the blood of the two breeds, so similar in all but size, nicking well.

Rabbit coursing took place in fields and paddocks—in fact anywhere where the dogs could have a clear two hundred yards run and there was room for the spectators and a public house at hand for refreshment. This far from sporting sport was killed by its own popularity, for the stakes became high enough to make cheating and dishonesty worth while. Rag racing lost its appeal with the arrival of Greyhound Tracks, but during its lifetime it was far better organised and administered than the older pastime. In rag racing five or six dogs ran in a heat. The 'slippers' stood behind the starting mark each holding a dog by the scruff or the tail: the 'walker-up' who was usually either the owner or trainer of the dog waved a rag in the face of their own dog and then, shouting encouragement, hurried up the course to the 'trig mark' which was placed some fifteen yards beyond the winning line. As the starter fired his pistol the slippers threw their dogs into their stride and the whole field raced to grip their own rag held outstretched to the side of their walker-up. Such was the grip of the dog and the force of his speed that he would be hoisted into the air like a fish on a line, for a racing Whippet can achieve a speed of between thirty and forty miles an hour.

The miners reared their dogs carefully; in fact, it was said, often more carefully than their own children.

Whippets first appeared at dog shows in the last years of the nineteenth century and one of the early exhibitors was Mr Fred Bottomley whose 'Chs. Manorley New Boy' and 'Manorley May' won on race grounds as well as in the show ring.

At the present time Whippets are extremely popular both as show and companion dogs, for they are not only good looking but are affectionate and intelligent. Their short, close and variously coloured coats and innately clean habits make them excellent house dogs, while their company can add a sporting interest to a country walk.

DESCRIPTION OF THE WHIPPET

His short, smooth coat requires no trouble, and he may be had in a wide variety of colours, such as black, red, white, brindle, fawn, blue, or mixtures of any of them. The ideal weight for the show dogs is 20 lb. for bitches and 21 lb. for dogs, height 17 in. for the one and 18½ in. for the other. The long and lean head is rather wide between the eyes, and flat at the top. The jaw powerful and clean cut. Eyes bright and fiery. The rose-shaped ears are small and fine in texture. The neck is long and muscular, elegantly arched, and free from throatiness. Shoulders sloping and muscular. Chest deep and roomy. Back broad and square, rather long, and slightly arched over the loins, which should be strong. Forelegs rather long, set well under the dog, and having a fair amount of bone. Hind-quarters strong and broad across. Stifles well bent, hocks well let down. Feet round. Tail long and tapering. Coat fine and close. The dog is obviously built for speed.

GUN DOGS

English Setters   Gordon Setters   Irish Setters

Pointers   German Short-haired Pointers

Curly-Coated Retrievers   Flat-Coated Retrievers

Golden Retrievers   Labrador Retrievers

Clumber Spaniels   Cocker Spaniels   Field Spaniels

Irish Water Spaniels   English Springer Spaniels

Welsh Springer Spaniels   Sussex Spaniels

Weimaraners

GUN DOGS

THE breeds that make up this section of the canine family need little or no explaining for their purpose in life is and always has been quite clear—to drive game from cover, to indicate where birds can be found and, with most of the breeds, to retrieve the game once it has been killed. The manner in which these dogs perform their work has naturally changed considerably since the time when a spaniel and a hawk were the essential possessions of a man of rank who would 'take' partridges and quail.

Spaniels are indeed the oldest of the 'gun dogs' and were with us long before the guns, for they are constantly mentioned from the time of Dame Juliana Berners and her *Boke of St Albans* (1486) onwards. What is more there is no gun dog breed in existence today which does not, in a greater or lesser degree, descend from the spaniel family.

Anyone interested in these early spaniels would probably do well to glance at that famous picture 'The Conversion of St Hubert' by the Master of Werden which can be seen in the National Gallery. The little dog drinking in the foreground is undoubtedly a typical spaniel of his time—small and low to ground and 'rough' of tail.

From the spaniel came the setter or 'Creeping Spaniel' as it was sometimes termed. As early as the thirteenth century these dogs were trained first to find the birds and then to drive them towards outstretched nets. Not much is heard of this type of work until the time of Robert Dudley, Earl of Northumberland, who is often but incorrectly credited with being the first man to train dogs for this purpose. John Caius mentions them again in his attempt to classify the dogs of his time for the benefit of Robert Gesner. By 1665 Gervase Markham writes: 'A setting dogge is a certaine lusty land spaniell taught by nature to hunt the partridges'.

The arrival of the sporting gun displaced the hawks and the nets. By 1700 Pointers had arrived in this country and although there is no reason to believe that they originally carried spaniel blood there are frequent mentions of their being crossed with the setters or 'setting dogges' after their arrival here.

The retriever breeds are the youngest branch of the gun dog family and their blood is extremely mixed and varied, but invariably either the Spaniel or the Setter plays some part in their ancestry.

Generally speaking all the gun dog breeds are docile, amenable, intelligent and anxious to please, and most are blessed with an ability to think for themselves. It is their charm and good sense that has made them such popular house dogs and companions, often to the neglect of their working ability.

English Setters

I T seems that the first mention of a Setter was made by Dr Johannes Caius in the year 1570. For the benefit of his friend Dr Gesner, for whom he was collecting information on the English dogs of the time, Dr Caius wrote a charming and, to us, amusing description of the work of the dog whom he called 'a Setter—or in Latin, Index'. Earlier writers, and some of the later ones, described these dogs as 'land spaniels' as opposed to water spaniels.

Taplin in his entertaining but somewhat pompous book *The Sportsman's Cabinet* devotes a chapter to 'The English Setter', a breed which he considered to be a cross between the Water or Springing Spaniel and the Pointer, but he makes no suggestion as to when the cross was made. The illustrations to this work were engravings from the paintings of that celebrated animal painter Philip Reinagle. The English Setter is easily recognisable as such, although he has a coarse head and wild expression not typical of the breed as it is today.

Throughout the nineteenth century it is easy to trace the English Setter's development. The old methods of killing game by hawking and netting had passed away and the custom of 'shooting flying', which had once been considered very questionable, had become a common practice; shooting driven birds was not yet usual but, in the main, a Setter's work had not altered much through the years.

It is to Mr Edward Laverack and Mr Purcell Llewellin that credit must be given for selective breeding from the various types and sizes of Setters that had been kept on various estates and, from them, evolving the lovely, graceful dog we know today.

Mr Laverack was a practical shooting man whose original pair of Setters 'Ponto' and 'Old Moll' came from a strain that claimed to have been kept pure for thirty-four years. Mr Laverack stuck closely to this line and always said that any attempted out-cross inevitably failed. In their hey-day the dogs of this strain were fine workers with great stamina. The term 'Laverack' became almost a breed name for Setters whose basic coat colouring was white. At Mr Laverack's death the dogs that remained in his kennel were sold before he was buried.

Overlapping in time the 'Laverack' strain were the dogs bred by Mr Purcell Llewellin and these also had a great run of success. Attempting to evolve his ideal Setter Mr Llewellin experimented with both the Gordon and Irish varieties, but eventually abandoned them for the English variety: considerable use was made of Laverack-bred bitches, but the previous close in-breeding was not resorted too. The Llewellin dogs scored many great successes both on the bench and in the field until the death of their owner in 1925 when Mr William Humphrey took over the kennel and his dogs still win well at Field Trials.

The practice of driving birds has made the use of Setters less general than it was formerly. Nevertheless, they are still successful at Field Trials, and are increasing in popularity as show and companion dogs. Unfortunately the types favoured in the field and on the bench differ considerably but, whether in the field or on the show bench, the English Setter is a dog of outstanding beauty and charming character.

DESCRIPTION OF THE ENGLISH SETTER

The dog is built on elegant lines, with a body of moderate length, well-laid shoulders and strong loins; slightly arched; all indicative of the power to gallop easily and last through a hard day's work. The legs, of course, must be beyond reproach, and the feet are close and compact and protected by hair between the toes. The neck is rather long, muscular, lean and slightly arched. There should be no dewlap. The brisket is deep and the ribs should be round, well sprung, with plenty of depth in the back ribs. The head is long and lean, with a well-defined stop. The skull is oval between the ears, with a well-defined occiput. The muzzle is moderately deep and fairly square. The dark hazel eyes are bright, mild, and intelligent. The ears, set on low, are of moderate length, and hang in folds close to the cheek. The tail should be carried almost on a line with the back. The coat is slightly wavy, long and silky, with plenty of feathering on legs and tail. There are various colours. The height should be about 26 in., the weight about 60 lb.

Gordon Setters

T HE Gordon Setter became a settled type during the nineteenth century when it was sometimes called the Black-and-Tan or Scotch Setter. To the fourth Duke of Gordon (1743-1827) goes the credit of being the originator of the breed, although he undoubtedly worked with the black, black-and-tan and tan-and-white Setters to be found in other kennels beside those housed in the kennels of Gordon Castle. It has often been suggested that the ducal breeding plans included the use of Bloodhounds—if this was so it would account for a number of things, both good and bad, in the make-up of the Gordon Setter. It would supply the answer to the question of why the Setters of this breed are apt to hunt with their heads held low to find scent on the ground instead of on the wind as a Setter should. It would also account for the heavy build of the dog and his colouring as well as a tendency to show the haw in the eye. For the other side of the coin it would give him determination in hunting and powers of endurance.

Another and somewhat scandalous story says that the old Duke was so impressed with the working ability of a Collie, owned by one of his shepherds, who could often find birds when the Setters had failed, that the old dog fathered several litters in the ducal kennels. Since no records were kept it is impossible to disentangle hard facts from mere gossip. After the Duke's death a sale of Setters was held in 1836 and the then very good price of 72 guineas was paid for 'Young Regent'.

By the beginning of the twentieth century Gordon Setters had deserted the Castle kennels, although they had become quite well known in the outer world.

A dog called 'Dandie', a direct descendant of the Gordon Castle dogs, had a part in one of the major rows that often took place in the unregenerate days of the early dog shows. The show, one of the first to be recorded, was held at the Corn Exchange, Newcastle, in 1859, and the exhibits were solely Setters and Pointers. The first prize was 'one of Papes celebrated double-barrelled guns worth £15 to £20'. When it appeared that the judge of Pointers owned the winning Setter 'Dandie', and the Setter judge owned the winning Pointer, the unsuccessful exhibitors were far from satisfied! The incident was, to some extent, responsible for the formation of the Kennel Club.

Other stories were whispered among the ranks of Gordon Setter exhibitors, but despite this unfortunate propaganda the breed forged ahead and was in great demand by shooting men in countries overseas. The breed's two best friends were firstly Mr Isaac Sharpe, a hard-headed businessman who made his living out of gun dogs and was always a strong supporter of the breed both in the ring and in the field: his 'Ch. Stylish Scorcher' and 'Stylish Ranger' were well known in both spheres. Secondly Mr R. Chapman whose 'Heather' prefix has adorned many famous Scottish Terriers and Gordon Setters.

The Gordon Setter is now climbing back into favour after a period in the doldrums. Not, perhaps, as fast a worker as the English Setter, but less flighty than his Irish relations, the Gordon is wise and sensible. In countries overseas retrieving is often added to his traditional work, and this makes him an excellent dual-purpose gun dog.

DESCRIPTION OF THE GORDON SETTER

The head of the Gordon is heavier than that of the English, being broad at the top, with a slightly rounded skull. From the well-developed occiput, the depth of the lower jaw is also greater. The nose is moderately long and broad and free from snipiness. Some show a slight haw and dewlap. Ears vary a good deal in length. The body, though heavier, is judged on similar lines to the English Setter, and legs and feet should be all that are looked for on a dog that is essentially a worker. There is plenty of feathering on legs and tail. The colouring adds greatly to the appearance. Formerly a tricolour, it is now a jet black, free from rustiness, and a rich dark mahogany tan, which is shown on the inside of the thighs, down the front of the stifle to the ground, and on the forelegs to the knees. The muzzle is also tan, and the spots over the eyes should be well defined.

47

Irish Setters

THE Irish Setter has not always had a coat of shining chestnut hue. During the last century red and white Setters were far more common, even in Ireland, than those of a solid colour. At the early shows, classes were provided for the parti-coloured varieties: today these are seen no more and all that remains is an occasional white patch on the chest of an otherwise solid coloured dog or a small white flash on the skull. This is known as the 'Palmerston snip'; a reminder of a famous ancestor and great sire, 'Ch. Palmerston' who ended his days in the United States and whose stuffed head hung for many years on the wall of a New York hotel.

It was probably due to the American craze for Irish or Red Setters that the breeding of these dogs was given such impetus in the last decade of the last century. One of the most famous of the Irish breeders was Miss Lidwell who lived near Dublin at a period when dog breeding was considered a most unwomanly pursuit. Mr Edward Laverack was anxious to buy Miss Lidwell's best dog 'Pluto', who was of perfectly pure Irish blood, but all his offers were met with scorn. A very surprised Mr Laverack returned to England dogless and 'Pluto' remained to improve the breed in his native land.

The Rev. Robert O'Callaghan who lived in Suffolk was one of the breed's strongest supporters on this side of the Irish Channel and his 'Brandeston' strain was as famous in the field as it was on the show bench and it was through the 'Brandestons' that Mrs Ingle Bepler founded her famous 'Rheola' kennel.

The 'Rheola' kennel was based on three bitches, 'Lady Honora', 'Ch. Carrig Maid' and 'Ch. Winifred' all of them descending from 'Ch. Palmerston'. 'Lady Honora' was the offspring of a brother and sister mating and was herself mated in turn to her father and her father's brother. Such close in-breeding, which continued for a number of years, produced a type that was recognisable anywhere and, furthermore, reproduced itself when mated to Setters of other strains. The 'Rheolas' had a wonderful career and many champions were bred in the kennel. There were numerous other successful breeders in those years before World War II—Sir Humphrey de Trafford, Mr Carbery, Sir Valentine Grace and Mrs Nagle. The latter is still an active supporter of the breed at Field Trials where her dogs have had many successes.

When dog breeding began again after the Second World War the Irish Setter breed faced a crisis that might well have brought about its extinction. The penalty for the long drawn out policy of in-breeding had to be paid, for it was discovered that at least one much used stud dog was responsible for transmitting the hereditary disease commonly known as 'night blindness', from which the victims lose their vision in a poor light and ultimately go completely blind. It was only by the most drastic tests and breeding regulations lasting over several years that the Irish Setter breed has largely been cleared and is now in a fair way to regaining its earlier popularity.

The character of the Irish Setter is truly Irish and filled with charm and humour. If well trained no breed is a better worker for they are fast and enthusiastic. The operative word in the education of these dogs is 'trained' and never 'broken' for they are highly sensitive as well as high spirited.

DESCRIPTION OF THE IRISH SETTER

Its body should be proportionate to its overall size with the ribs well sprung, leaving plenty of lung room and with the loins muscular and slightly arched. The haunches should be wide and powerful and the shoulders deep and sloping well back. The chest should be as deep as possible, and the front rather narrow without suggesting lack of lung room. The neck should be moderately long, very muscular, not too thick and free from any throatiness. The forelegs should be straight and sinewy, well-boned and with elbows well let down and not inclined either in or out. The hindlegs should be long and muscular. The head is on the same general lines as those of the other varieties of setters but is not so heavy as the Gordon's. Neither is the lip so square nor the stop so pronounced as in the other two varieties. Yet the muzzle should be moderately deep and fairly square at the end and the stop should be well marked, the length of foreface from stop to nose being the same as that of skull from stop to occiput which should be well defined. The head should be free from coarseness and the skull oval from ear to ear with plenty of brain room. The coat should be of moderate length, as flat as possible and of a rich chestnut colour; small white markings on toes, head, and chest are permitted. The eyes should be dark hazel or dark brown and the nose dark mahogany, dark walnut or black.

Pointers

ONE is apt to think of the Pointer as a pure, dyed-in-the-wool British breed. In fact the Pointer was all but unknown in this country before 1700 when one or two were brought into this country, probably from Portugal. The Pointer had been known on the Continent, mainly in Spain, for a long time before its adoption here. It seems possible that there were two types—the heavily built Spanish Pointers and a lighter variety, which were probably French or Italian. The portrait of 'The Duke of Kingston with his Pointers', dated 1725, shows elegantly built animals, whereas all descriptions of Spanish Pointers describe them as being heavily built with massive heads; this is borne out by the Stubbs picture engraved by Woollet in 1768.

The Spanish type seems to have had only a limited reign in this country and the lighter or so-called English Pointers soon superseded a dog that was found to be so slow and so heavy that it rapidly became exhausted, although it was as steady as a rock when on point.

Colonel Thornton is usually held responsible for producing the English Pointer by means of crossing the Spanish breed with a Foxhound. This certainly produced a more shapely and more active dog with excellent feet and a capacity for work, but it also produced a dog who was apt to search for scent on the ground instead of holding his head high to find it on the wind. The greatest of all champions of the Pointer and one who did much for the breed was William Arkwright, whose book *The Pointer and its Predecessors* is now an almost unobtainable canine classic.

In the early part of the twentieth century Pointers were fortunate in their owners, most of whom required their dogs to be dual-purpose and were careful to retain the substance necessary for a worker, while achieving the refinement and quality desirable in a show winner. Mr Isaac Sharpe's 'Stylish' dogs had a considerable influence on the breed: dogs and bitches from this kennel were usually leased to various large shoots and moors during the shooting season and returned to their owner during the spring and summer when they either appeared at shows or undertook their maternal duties.

During the years that immediately preceded the last war it was found necessary to bring in fresh blood. Of these importations one was the Belgian-bred bitch who became 'Field Trial Champion Blackfield Gill' and another the Italian dog 'Gaff di San Patrick' who was an excellent sire. This pair produced two Field Trial champions and 'Banchory Jack', a great notability of his time. After the war the breed was still further improved and strengthened by further importations.

As working dogs Pointers are not in such great demand as they were, but the breed has a good record at Field Trials. There is an increasing interest in their breeding and exhibiting and the breed registrations are rising steadily year by year. Mrs W. Parkinson's bitch 'Ch. Chiming Bells' was the best exhibit at Cruft's Show in 1958 and there is a good demand for British bred stock from various parts of the world; on the whole the breed and its owners can pride themselves on being in an extremely good position. One would like to see more dogs with the typical 'dish' face and there are signs that breeders are doing their best to restore this characteristic.

DESCRIPTION OF THE POINTER

There must be a lot of power in the body, which should carry plenty of muscle. Ribs deep and carried well back, so that there is no weakness of loin. Thighs are long and muscular, and stifles long and well bent. The head is long and has a well-pronounced stop between the eyes. The large eyes betoken animation and intelligence. The ears of medium length, should be thin and silky and set high. The neck is long and muscular and well placed at the shoulders, which should be fine and sloping. The body colour is principally white, and the colour of the markings is not of much importance, though, perhaps, liver-and-white are most popular.

German Short-haired Pointers

THE German Short-haired Pointer, as his full style and title implies, came to us from Germany and Austria where these dogs have been bred for a number of years and are very popular. Their main claim to superiority over our more familiar shooting dogs—the Spaniels, the Setters, the Pointers and the Retrievers—is based on their claim that they can do the work of all three—hunt, point and retrieve. Whether there has yet been a dog that can do all three jobs with the style and finish of a well-trained specialist has not yet been conclusively proved. But there is no doubt that an intelligent Short-haired Pointer makes a handy dog for the rough shoot and for the owner who does not want to keep more than one dog.

The history of this German gun dog is relatively brief. In the seventeenth century a number of Spanish Pointers found their way from Spain to the regions that are now Germany and earned considerable praise for their ability as shooting dogs—just as they did on their arrival in this country. The Germans, however, decided that they wanted a tracking dog as well as a gun dog and crossed their Pointers with Bloodhounds and thus produced a heavy, slow-moving dog with which they were well satisfied. History does not relate whether these cross-breds hunted as a Pointer or a Setter should, holding their heads high to catch the scent on the wind, or whether they worked like a Bloodhound, taking up the scent from the ground. When Field Trials became popular some sixty years ago the Continental dogs could not hold a candle to our British-bred and speedier, more racily-built dogs. In consequence further crosses were made with English Pointers who themselves carried some Foxhound blood. Broadly speaking this amalgamation of various breeds produced what was required and a few generations of selective breeding produced a uniformity of type and a new breed was born and christened 'Deutsche Kurzaar'. The emphasis on the short hair seems unnecessary since all the breeds involved were, and always had been, short-haired. The term may have arisen to distinguish these dogs from the Wire-haired Pointing Griffons who were being developed for much the same purpose at much the same time.

The United States accepted the Short-haired Pointer earlier than Great Britain where it was not much seen until 1948 and 1949. The German Short-haired Pointer Club was formed in 1951. Since then the breed has made slow but steady progress, especially since owners and breeders have dropped the somewhat dictatorial attitude to the training and breeding of these dogs which they adopted at first, an attitude which offended many of those who might have given the breed support earlier. The breed has had championship status since 1955 and makes good entries at shows. There has been considerable improvement in general soundness and at Field Trials several dogs have competed creditably. But there are anomalies to be overcome before this pleasant and amiable breed can obtain the highest working honours.

DESCRIPTION OF THE GERMAN SHORT-HAIRED POINTER

The weight of a fully grown dog is generally between 55 and 70 lb. and the height 23 to 25 in. Bitches should be 10 lb. lighter and 2 in. smaller than dogs. The coat may be solid liver, liver and white spotted, or liver and white ticked; colours other than liver and white are not permitted. The tail is docked to two-fifths of the original length. The German Short-haired Pointer will point, hunt or retrieve.

Curly-Coated Retrievers

THE Curly-Coated Retriever is the oldest of the retriever breeds and at the present time the least popular. The fortunes of the breed have always been either up or down and at the time of writing they appear to be rising once again.

During the nineteenth century sportsmen's habits changed and Setters and Pointers were no longer expected to retrieve and Spaniels not only had their own work but were not always large enough or fast enough to do the job: in consequence some other variety of dog had to be evolved. The Curly-Coated Retriever was the first specialist to offer. There is no known record of where, how or at whose instigation the Curly breed came into existence—it would seem that, like Topsy, he just grow'd. A guess that is as good as any, suggests that the Water Dog—now a lost variety, but often praised in early canine literature for its intelligence and working ability—who should not be confused with the smaller Water Spaniel, was crossed with an early Irish Water Spaniel whose antecedents are also somewhat mysterious. One has only to compare the two breeds to see the obvious similarities—the tightly-curled coat, head structure and body shape. The Curly Retriever although usually black is perfectly acceptable if liver coloured. It is not impossible to believe that the Poodle may have been involved in the matter.

The arguments in favour of the Curly Retrievers were many, for when well trained they were tireless workers with excellent noses, good water dogs and the close but curly coat was almost impervious to water, although inclined to catch in brambles. Keepers liked these dogs because they made excellent guards and were always on the alert and not ready to be friendly with all and sundry.

Curly-Coated Retrievers first appeared at shows in 1860 and in due course a club was formed to further breed interests, but by 1890 this variety was losing ground to the Flat-Coated Retriever who, in its turn, lost to the Labrador and Golden Retrievers.

By 1914, when dog breeding ceased for the war years, the annual registrations were a mere fifty-three dogs. Between the First and the Second World Wars the breed gained the support of Brigadier Lance and his wife and the 'Sarona' prefix that had become famous as a hall mark for Salukis often appeared on Curly-Coated Retrievers, while Mrs Ackerley's 'Ackrow' kennel was very prominent for several years. There was a notable increase in show entries and several dogs made successful appearances at Field Trials. The breed appeared to be on or nearing the crest of a wave but it was dashed on the rocks by the outbreak of the Second World War. Nevertheless, there were ninety registrations in 1946, but in succeeding years the totals declined again despite the continued support of Brigadier Lance whose show dogs were always also workers. Dogs and bitches from his kennel have undoubtedly left a permanent mark on the breed.

The future of the oldest of the Retriever breeds still appears extremely uncertain which seems a pity. The Curly-Coated Retriever may have faults, but he also has many virtues for he is a one-man dog with great devotion to his master, and is potentially a good honest worker.

DESCRIPTION OF THE CURLY-COATED RETRIEVER

The head is long, well-proportioned, the skull not too flat jaws strong but not inclined to snipiness. The eyes are black or brown, rather large but not too prominent. The ears are rather small, set on low, lying close to the head and covered with short curls. The neck is moderately long with deep muscular shoulders well laid back. The hindquarters are also strong and muscular, hocks low to the ground, with moderate bend to stifle and hock. The tail is moderately short, tapering towards the point, carried fairly straight and covered with curls. The coat is a mass of crisp curls all over and the colour should be black or liver. The weight is 70 to 80 lb. and the height at shoulder is approximately 26 in.

55

Flat-Coated Retrievers

IT is not so many years ago that one heard as much of Wavy-Coated Retrievers as one did of Flat-Coated Retrievers and one was apt to think of them as two separate breeds. This was not unnatural since it was as Wavy-Coated Retrievers that these dogs first appeared in the Kennel Club Stud Book. At the present time there is no differentiation and the approved coat is one that is as flat as possible and the official title of the breed is 'Retriever (Flat-Coated)'.

Like the Curly-Coated Retriever the Flat Coat evolved at a time in the nineteenth century when it became fashionable to have a separate dog to collect the shot game and not expect the job to be done by Setters, Pointers or Spaniels. The new custom probably arose because the improved guns of the period made the game bags fuller and it became impossible to expect a dog to carry out two jobs with equal success.

There has never been much doubt about the main breeds used to produce the flat-coated dogs—the Setter being the root stock; for his hereditary instincts were enough to give him a good start for the new style of work. Grafted on to this well-established line was the Newfoundland, a breed that had been coming into this country since the eighteenth century and was strongly built and an excellent water dog who had often been used as a retriever of fish and game in his native land. Somewhere along the line there may have been an infusion of Labrador blood, although the breed was not very numerous in those days.

Naturally it took more than one generation of cross-breeding to produce a completely suitable Retriever that, in its turn, would reproduce itself. Perhaps the greatest difficulty encountered was the exclusion of the Setter head with its well-defined occiput as well as the frequent production of dogs that were heavy, coarse or too large.

The first classes for 'Wavy-Coated Retrievers' were scheduled at a London show in 1864 and won by 'Wyndham' owned by Mr T. Meyrick, M.P. Throughout the latter half of the last century the Flat-Coats were very popular and for the improvement that took place thanks must go to Mr S. E. Shirley, M.P., a founder of the Kennel Club, who was interested in several breeds. Another great supporter of these Retrievers was Mr. Harding Cox whose 'Black' strain produced many notable dogs. Reading the history of those old days it is apparent that the leading breeders, owners and exhibitors were keen and practical sportsmen who used their dogs for the purpose for which they were intended. Furthermore, their breeding plans placed emphasis on the physical attributes that they considered necessary in a working dog.

From about 1903 onward the Flat-Coat lost ground to the Labrador Retriever and the Golden Retriever. Nevertheless, it still had and has today some staunch supporters and remains a good sound working dog as well as being a very handsome one. His kindly nature is apparent from his gentle expression and the quiet dignity of his bearing. Most of the outstanding show winners gain the working award that gains them the title of Champion.

DESCRIPTION OF THE FLAT-COATED RETRIEVER

The head is long and nicely moulded, with practically no stop, being level in line from nose to occiput. The occiput is not accentuated, the skull forming a curve where it joins the neck. The eyes are small, dark and kindly. Body fairly short. Front legs absolutely straight, with fair bone. Feet round and strong. Stifles and hocks well bent, the latter being placed low. Tail short. The outer coat should be perfectly flat, not wavy, with feathering on thighs, tail and front legs. Colour black or liver. In every respect the dog must be put together on lines that permit of easy movement and endurance. The weight should be between 60 and 70 lb.

Golden Retrievers

THE Golden Retriever has beauty, charm, intelligence and is willing to adapt himself to whatever station in life his fate may decree. He is an excellent and honest worker in the field and as a companion he is charming, sagacious and intelligent. It is notable that a very large number of dogs of this breed have been dual champions—champions on the show bench and champions in the field.

For many years the Golden Retriever was said to have originated in Russia and there was a detailed story that recounted how Sir Dudley Marjoribanks, later Lord Tweedmouth, bought a whole troupe of Russian dogs that he saw performing in a circus at Brighton in 1858. He is said to have despatched these dogs to his Scottish estate Guisachan for use as retrievers and for tracking wounded deer. In due course, said the story, these dogs were out-crossed to a sandy-coloured Bloodhound and possibly some other type of retrieving dog and thus became the ancestors of the modern Golden Retriever. This story, with variations of detail, was pretty widely accepted by canine writers, and with some reluctance by the more experienced breeders of Retrievers. To support the story was the fact that dogs known as Russian Setters and Russian Retrievers had been seen in this country during the nineteenth century and are mentioned and described by several of the canine writers of the period. In 1952, however, new facts emerged and Lord Tweedmouth's great-nephew, the sixth Earl of Ilchester who died in 1961, disclosed in an article that his ancestor had kept a detailed record of his breeding operations between the years 1835 and 1890. From this stud book it was learnt that Lord Tweedmouth had bought a yellow Wavy-Coated Retriever at Brighton in 1865. This dog, 'Nous' by name, went to Guisachan where he was later mated to 'Belle', a Tweed Water Spaniel—a now unknown type of retrieving dog mentioned on various occasions by early nineteenth-century writers as an excellent working dog who resembled a small, brown or liver-coloured retriever. The mating resulted in four yellow bitch puppies being born in 1868. From this account it would appear that all Golden Retrievers of today descend from this litter.

Lord Ilchester's account sounds very factual and detailed but there are various factors that make one wonder whether the old stud book told the whole tale and that there may not have been at least a germ of truth concealed in the earlier story.

Whoever their ancestors may have been the Yellow or Golden Retriever breed flourished and increased. These dogs became increasingly popular and began to appear both at Field Trials as well as at shows. The Golden Retriever Club was founded in 1911 and the breed given its own Kennel Club register in 1913. Once the 1914-1918 war was over progress was steady and the breed won many admirers in both spheres of its activity. Mrs Charlesworth was a great supporter of the breed and her dog 'Noranby Campfire' was the first dog to qualify as a champion.

At the present time the Golden Retriever is the second most popular of all the Retrievers and gives place in the gun dog group only to the Labrador Retriever and the Cocker Spaniel.

DESCRIPTION OF THE GOLDEN RETRIEVER

The coat of the Golden Retriever may be flat or wavy, but never curly. The colour should be any shade of gold or cream. The body is well balanced and short coupled, and deep through the heart. Shoulders well laid back, and long in the blade. Feet round and cat-like. The skull is broad, muzzle powerful and wide. Weak jaws are objectionable. The eyes, which should be placed wide apart, are dark golden or brown, and have a kindly expression. The weight should be between 55 and 70 lb., the height between 20 and 24 in.

Labrador Retrievers

THROUGHOUT the nineteenth century one finds a number of references to Labrador Retrievers as well as 'St John's Dogs' and 'Lesser Labradors', but of their size or how they differed in appearance we know very little.

It has always been clearly understood that the earliest dogs from Labrador came to this country in the trading vessels that plied, generally with cargoes of fish, between that country and Poole in Dorset. The seamen who brought these dogs over found a ready market for them with the sportsmen of this country since they were hardy and intelligent and made excellent gun dogs. They had to be tough since the Labrador fishermen used their dogs for retrieving fish that had escaped from the hooks and nets, while the settlers used them for retrieving the wild duck they shot on the rocky, wave-beaten shores. Even in winter a working dog might well be in and out of icy water twenty times in a day.

The increasing number of dogs arriving in the fishermen's boats could not fail to arouse the interest of the customs officials; the bribing of them became an expensive business and it soon ceased to be worth while to bring dogs over in the old speculative way. It was not very long, however, before sportsmen on this side of the Atlantic began arranging for dogs to be sent over to them. As early as 1870 we find recorded in the Kennel Club Stud Book 'Lion', alias 'Hercules' and the bitch 'Bess', both stated to be imported Labradors and who became the parents of Mr S. E. Shirley's 'Paris' who was also sometimes known as 'Lion'.

The earliest serious breeders of Labradors were the second Lord Malmesbury, the fifth Duke of Buccleuch, Lord John Scott, the tenth Earl of Home and the Hon. A. Holland Hibbert who later became Lord Knutsford.

Among the very earliest prize winners after the Kennel Club officially acknowledged the breed in 1903 were the Hon. A. Holland Hibbert's 'Munden Sovereign' and 'Munden Sentry', while two years later 'Munden Sentry' was one of the first of his breed to attract attention at a Field Trial. From then on successes at both Trials and shows were frequent. From 1907 until 1914 progress was rapid—Major Portal's 'Flapper' became the breed's first Field Trial Champion; 'Peter', 'Patron' and 'Percy of Faskally' were all notable winners and so was 'Field Trial Champion Peter of Whitmore'. About 1914 we hear the first hint of the 'Banchory' kennel owned by Mrs Quintin Dick who afterwards became Lorna, Countess Howe. The Banchory kennel housed many notable dogs in its time but none more remarkable than 'Banchory Bolo'. This dog was bought as a rogue for the sake of his breeding but after a serious illness, during which he was nursed by his mistress, he became a changed character—not only a devoted companion but a dual champion and a famous sire. King George V was a great lover of a Labrador and his 'Wolferton' dogs sometimes appeared at shows, although they were mainly valued as workers.

Today the Labrador breed seems to have an unassailable position as the most popular of the retrievers and, since they are wise and sensible, they make excellent companions both in the home and in the field.

60

DESCRIPTION OF THE LABRADOR RETRIEVER

The coat is short, dense, free from wave, with a weather-resisting undercoat, and altogether distinctive. The colour is generally black, chocolate or yellow. The wide skull affords plenty of room for the brain. There is a slight stop, and the head is clean-cut without any fleshiness of cheeks. The jaws are long, powerful, and devoid of either snipiness or of exaggeration in length. The eye may be brown or hazel. Neck long and powerful. Shoulders long and sloping. Chest should be of good width and depth. The tail is very characteristic, having a peculiar rounded appearance, from which it is known as an 'otter' tail. Thick towards the base, it tapers gradually to the tip, is of medium length, and has practically no feathering, but is clothed thickly all round with a short, dense coat. The height should be between $21\frac{1}{2}$ and $22\frac{1}{2}$ in.

Clumber Spaniels

THE Clumber Spaniel is an odd man out in the Spaniel family. With the other Spaniel breeds it is always possible to perceive the link that joins one breed to another. No trace of Spaniels with any resemblance to those given by the Duc de Noailles to the second Duke of Newcastle, who established them at Clumber in the eighteenth century, has been found here, nor have Continental canine historians been particularly helpful. It seems likely, therefore, that these dogs were a private strain owned by the de Noailles family and that for some reason the Duc transferred all the dogs in his kennel to the Duke of Newcastle. In 1788 Francis Wheatley, R.A., painted 'The Return from Shooting' which shows the Duke of Newcastle, Colonel Litchfield, the head keeper and three Clumber Spaniels who greatly resemble the dogs one knows today. It is generally believed that the three dogs in the picture were some of the original dogs from the de Noailles kennel.

For a number of years the Clumber breed of Spaniel was unknown outside the kennels of a very few shooting men living in the neighbourhood of Clumber who had received them as gifts from the Newcastle family, but with the coming of dog shows in the nineteenth century the breed began to compete in Spaniel classes. In the first volumes of the Kennel Club Stud Book a number of Clumbers appear. One of the earliest was Mr R. S. Holford's dog 'Trimbush' who did some winning in 1861 and 1862 and became the sire of 'Duchess' bred by the Rev. T. Pearce (Idstone) and who is said to have been sold to H.R.H. the Prince of Wales, afterwards Edward VII. It is not impossible that it was from the descendants of this bitch that King George V got his fondness for the breed since during his lifetime there were always a number of good working Clumbers in the royal kennels. These dogs usually worked as a team and were of excellent type as is proved by the fact that they were frequent winners at the larger dogs shows. The royal Clumbers were sold after the death of King George V and some of the dogs became the property of the late Baroness Burton of Dochfour who was interested in the breed for a short while.

Despite an excellent record at Field Trials the popularity of Clumber Spaniels began to decline during the second decade of the present century. Various quite feasible reasons have been given for this—Clumbers are not the easiest of dogs to rear if they are to grow up sound and straight limbed. They need the best of food and experienced care in puppyhood; when adults they need still further care and much exercise to keep them from running to fat. When at work they need to drink frequently and, furthermore, methods of shooting have changed and many shooting men need a faster worker than the slow, solid and heavily-built Clumber Spaniel.

Of recent years there has been a slight sign of increasing interest in these very attractive dogs. There was a movement on foot to popularise the use of a team of Clumbers in the place of beaters, but after some early success this idea seems to have faded away. Today the Clumber appears at only the leading dog shows, where about twenty usually keep the breed flag flying.

In character the Clumber is less demonstrative and more dignified than the other Spaniels, but it is to be hoped that they will never be allowed to entirely disappear from our midst.

62

DESCRIPTION OF THE CLUMBER SPANIEL

He may be described as a heavy, square, massive animal, with a thoughtful expression. The weight of a dog may be from 55 to 70 lb. The long and heavy body stands on short straight legs; the chest is wide and deep, and shoulders strong and muscular. Hindquarters very powerful and well developed. Neck thick and powerful and well feathered underneath. Back straight, broad and long. Head large, square and massive, of medium length, broad on top, with a decided occiput. Heavy brows with a deep stop; heavy muzzle and deep flews. The eyes are dark amber, slightly sunk, and show the haw. The stern, set low and well feathered, is carried about level with the back. The coat is abundant, short and straight, and the colour is plain white with lemon markings. Slight head markings with white body are preferred.

63

Cocker Spaniels

THE Cocker Spaniels could well adopt 'Ubique' as their motto for they are almost universally popular; no dog can better adapt itself to circumstances and be all things to any man without losing an iota of its characteristic charm or affection for its owner. It is this very adaptability and popularity that have led to the Cocker becoming more of a companion than a gun dog. The instincts are still there—the young offspring of a string of show champions will fetch his thrown plaything and return with it and he will use his nose to find such desirable things as are hidden from him—it is the dogs' owners who do not recognise or will not train the deep-seated instincts of the breed to a useful purpose.

The history of the Cocker Spaniels as an independent breed is not a very long one. Nevertheless, small Spaniels have been used for work on rough land with thick, low covert for a very long time. Although they can and will retrieve, the true work of such Spaniels is to push out game for the guns. The term Cocker or Cocking Spaniel appears in many early sporting works. About 1859, when dog shows first began, Clumber Spaniels usually had a separate classification, while the others took pot luck under the heading of 'Spaniels, other breeds used for sporting purposes'. Their pedigrees were recorded as 'Spaniels, Field, Cocker and Sussex', with separate lists for Irish Water Spaniels and Water Spaniels. By 1870 we hear only of Field Spaniels, who were divided into two categories of over and under 25 lb. in weight. It was twenty-three years later that the Kennel Club gave the smaller variety of Spaniels a register of its own and even then each dog had to be weighed before entering the judging ring to ensure that it was in fact under 25 lb. This rigid rule handicapped breeders and restricted progress, since dogs and bitches of good type, but possibly a little overweight, were only too often neglected as breeding possibilities in favour of weedy specimens. Furthermore, the rule was often evaded and a border line dog could be a Cocker in the morning and appear, replete with a good meal, as a Field in the afternoon. The Spaniel Club, which had been in existence since 1885, campaigned for nearly sixteen years before the rule was abolished. In 1901 the Cocker Spaniel as a completely separate breed was launched and a year later its specialist club was formed. From this time forward the breed has never looked back.

Some years before the above events took place—in 1879—the black dog 'Ch. Obo', the Adam from whom all present-day Cockers whatever their colour descend, appeared in the show ring. He was a rather strange looking animal to modern eyes, long in the body and short in the neck and legs, but his name will be forever remembered.

Most of the famous early strains were dual purpose—the 'Rivingtons', the 'Brutons', the 'Braesides' and the 'Doonys'. So were most of those owned by Mr R. Lloyd, whose son, Mr H. S. Lloyd, has carried on what his father began and made the 'of Ware' affix famous in all the many countries where Cockers are appreciated. The number of Cockers registered in recent years has been astounding and not altogether beneficial to the breed. In 1939, 5,372 dogs were registered; in 1947, the total was 27,000, a record for any breed. At the present time with registrations around the six thousand mark the breed is in a far healthier and happier position.

DESCRIPTION OF THE COCKER SPANIEL

The weight should be between 25 and 28 lb., and within that compass should be compressed a good deal of power. The back not being quite so long as in other varieties of Spaniels, the dog looks more compact and firmly knit. The legs, which have plenty of bone, and are feathered and straight, should be sufficiently short for concentrated power, but not too short to interfere with full activity. Feet firm, round, and cat-like. The neck is long, strong and muscular. Shoulders sloping and fine; chest deep and well developed, but not too wide. Back and loins immensely strong and compact in proportion to size. The stern should never be carried higher than in a line with the back, and the lower its carriage and action the better. The coat is flat and silky in texture, with sufficient feather, but not too profuse and never curly. The skull and forehead should be well developed; ears lobular, set low and well clothed with hair.

Field Spaniels

FROM the moment the Cocker Spaniel and the Field Spaniel breeds parted company the former has rapidly improved in popularity and type, while the latter has slowly receded into the background and is now in a very parlous state.

In the last years of the last century coloured Field Spaniels were kept somewhat apart from the black Field Spaniels—quite understandably since the solid coloured Cockers of today are seldom crossed with the parti-colours except under exceptional circumstances. It was the black Field Spaniels who fared worst at the hands of fanciers who had no interest in the breed's working capabilities and were interested purely from the exhibition point of view.

It has been generally accepted that a Spaniel should be low on the leg in order to work through and below undergrowth and drive game towards the guns. He was not generally required to retrieve. As one can see by glancing at the history of the modern Cocker, the two breeds were very closely linked. In fact the only difference between the Field and the Cocker was one of size and it was far from uncommon for dogs from the same litter to compete as different breeds. Once the Cocker became an independent breed he became a compact, short-backed and active little dog. The Field Spaniel on the other hand became longer and longer in the back as he became shorter and shorter on his heavily-boned legs and it was not long before he was completely unfitted to be considered as a working breed and his appearance greatly resembled that of a sausage.

It was between 1890 and 1900 that this craze for length of body reached its height of absurdity and exhibitors could be seen stretching out their dogs while the judge debated which of the two was half-an-inch longer than the other. The two longest animals of the period were said to be 'Undeniable' and 'Rother Queen'.

The most prominent breeder at the turn of the century was Mr Moses Woolland whose 'Bridford' kennel housed both Sussex and black Field Spaniels, and turned out a long line of winners including 'Ch. Bridford Boy', 'Bridford Brilliant', Bridford Tommy', 'Gypsey' and quite a number more. Another well-known kennel which was successful in the field as well as in the show ring was that owned by Mr H. E. Gray. By 1905 the breed was diminishing in numbers but improving in appearance. But the Cocker and the Springer Spaniels had far outstripped their heavier brethren and the Field Spaniels continued to recede into the background.

Several efforts have been made to revive interest and prevent the breed from dying out altogether and for a short while there appeared to be hope, but at the time of writing there are probably not more than a dozen dogs in this country.

It will be a pity if a dog with such a pleasant character is allowed to disappear, for the Fields are very affectionate and devoted to those who own them.

DESCRIPTION OF THE FIELD SPANIEL

Field Spaniels should weigh between 35 and 50 lb. and stand about 18 in. at the shoulder. The flat or slightly waved coat should be black, liver, golden liver, mahogany red, roan, or any of these colours with tan marks over the eyes, on the cheeks, feet and pasterns. On the chest, under the belly and behind the legs there should be abundant feather. Skull well developed, long and lean with great length of muzzle. Ears moderately long and wide, set low and feathered. Eyes dark. Neck long and muscular. Shoulders long, sloping and well set back. Body of moderate length with strong loin and deep chest. Hindquarters strong and muscular. Feet round with strong pads. Tail well set on and carried low.

67

Irish Water Spaniels

THE Irish Water Spaniel is an individualist among the Spaniels for he bears very little outward resemblance to the rest of the family.

The history of the Irish Water Spaniel really begins in 1834 when Mr McCarthy's 'Boatswain' was born. There had been Water Spaniels in Ireland at an earlier date, but very little is known of them or their appearance. There was the 'St Leger breed', a strain kept at Crom Castle, Co. Fermanagh, and the Northern Water Spaniel, whom that eminent authority Colonel Claude Cane believed to be very similar to the curly-coated English Water Spaniels now seen no more. Mr McCarthy never offered any explanation of how his Southern Irish Water Spaniels came into existence, but they undoubtedly bred true and suggestions that Poodles or Curly-Coated Retrievers might have formed part of the breed background have never been disproved.

Irish Water Spaniels first appeared at a show held in Birmingham in 1862 when Mr Dunderdale's 'Charlie' and Mr C. E. N. Lloyd's 'Bell' were the winners and nothing is known about their pedigrees. But since 'Boatswain' lived to be eighteen, he was the progenitor of nearly all the dogs and bitches whose names appear in the first volume of the Kennel Club Stud Book, while it is through his son 'Jack' and his grandson 'Ch. Blair' that most of the outstanding dogs of the late eighteenth century and early nineteenth century descend. In fact, it is improbable that there is any dog of the breed alive today who could not find 'McCarthy's Boatswain' among his ancestors.

As a working dog the Irish Water Spaniel was, and still is, excellent. He is a wild fowler's dog pure and simple—too large and too curly coated for working through undergrowth. But there is no water too wet or too cold for him to plunge into and retrieve a fallen duck. The somewhat oily coat typical of the breed is almost impervious to water and dries quickly.

The Irish Water Spaniel is at his best when he is trained from early youth by one understanding master who appreciates his Irish charm, sense of humour and occasional obstinacy, yet can maintain discipline and develop the very high degree of intelligence that lies beneath the dog's curly pate.

The first club to be founded for the purpose of encouraging the breeding of Irish Water Spaniels came into being in 1890 but in 1926 the Irish Water Spaniel Association was founded and both bodies support shows and organise trials for working dogs. The 1920s and 1930s were the hey-day of the breed for then it gained popularity in European countries as well as in the United States and Canada. The last war, of course, put a stop to progress and the Irishman has never regained the ground then lost. In Eire, however, the breed has a very staunch supporter in Mrs Barrington whose 'Brittas' kennel has produced some excellent dogs that often compete on this side of the Irish Channel.

It is difficult to understand why a dog of such intelligence and endearing clownishness should not become more widely appreciated.

DESCRIPTION OF THE IRISH WATER SPANIEL

In general appearance the Irish Water Spaniel is a short-backed, upstanding, strongly-made dog measuring from 20 to 23 in. at shoulder. Clad in a coat of short, crisp curls, neither woolly nor wiry, and of a rich shade of liver-puce. The head is capacious and not too narrow, and is surmounted by a top-knot of long, curly hair coming right down between the eyes to a peak, leaving the temples and face quite smooth; this, with a peculiar length of foreface and a deep, square muzzle, eyes comparatively small, dark brown or hazel in colour, give it a quaint and very intelligent appearance. The forelegs straight and are abundantly covered with long curls, somewhat shorter in front than at the back. Long stifles and low-set hocks are characteristic, the latter, well covered with hair at the back, should be smooth in front downwards. The tail is short and smooth except for about 4 in. at the root which should be covered with close curls. The ears are very long, low-set and covered with long twisted curls. The gait differs from that of any other variety of Spaniel.

English Springer Spaniels

ALTHOUGH the English Springer Spaniel was admitted to the Kennel Club registers only as recently as 1902 he is a type of land Spaniel that has been known both here and on the Continent for several hundred years. Dogs of this type appear in several well-known paintings by old masters, among the most notable being 'A Flemish Wedding Feast' by Jan Steen, and 'The Sleeping Sportsman' by Metsu, while Philip Reinagle shows a very typical Springer flushing a woodcock in engravings illustrated in *The Sportsman's Cabinet* (1803). Taplin, who compiled *The Sportsman's Cabinet*, writing of the 'Springing Spaniel' remarks that: 'They are nearly two-fifths less in height and strength than the Setter: delicately formed, ears long, soft and pliable, coat waving and silky, eyes and nose red or black, the tail somewhat bushy and pendulous, always in motion when actively employed'.

The sorting of various types of land and water Spaniels into breeds was one of the difficult tasks that had to be faced by the Spaniel Club and the Kennel Club late in the nineteenth century and early in the twentieth. Getting ducklings into baskets must have been a simple task in comparison for no sooner had they decided on the desired appearance and characteristics for one breed than it was found that many of the animals who most closely approached the proposed blue-print were by or out of dogs of some other breed, while their litter brothers and sisters were award winners in classes for yet another variety. Getting these matters settled took quite a long time since the branches of the Spaniel family tree are so closely intertwined: even the well known early Springer dog 'Ch. Rivington Sam' owned an unregistered dog called 'Sport' as a sire and an accepted Cocker bitch 'Rivington Ribbon' as his dam!

For a short while and by the wish of the Spaniel Club the Springer Spaniel was known as the Norfolk Spaniel, but there was a great deal of bad feeling about the name. Nobody appeared to be able to trace any connection between the dogs and the county and only a very vague one with the ducal family and there was something of an impasse. In consequence, the breed was deleted from the Club's classification for some time. However, in 1902 the Kennel Club accepted the title of Springer Spaniel and divided it into two types—the English and the Welsh.

The first classes confined to Springers were judged by Mr W. Arkwright and the earliest winner was Mr Winton Smith's liver and white dog 'Beechgrove Will'. Another very practical gun dog man who was quick to show a constructive interest in the breed was Mr Isaac Sharpe whose 'Stylish' dogs were so well known.

Progress in those early years was slow but sure and most of the dogs were truly dual purpose. About 1905 Mr Eversfield bought 'Ch. Velox Powder' from Sir Thomas Boughey who claimed that his strain had been in his family for a hundred years. 'Velox Powder's' limited number of show appearances were quite creditable but as a worker and sire of workers he became a pillar of the breed. The 'O'Vara' dogs were another strain who at a somewhat later date carried on the working tradition of the breed.

At the present time the Springer remains the favourite Spaniel of those who like a good companion who, when required, can do a good day's work in the field.

DESCRIPTION OF THE ENGLISH SPRINGER

Weighing about 50 lb., about 20 in. in height, the English Springer is big enough to retrieve comfortably. The straight, strong legs should be nicely feathered and of a practical length. The body is well ribbed-up to a strong loin, and is of medium length. The back is straight or slightly arched. Excessive length and lowness should be penalised as destroying the balance and rendering him less suited for his work. The shoulders are sloping and free, the chest deep and well developed. The head, which denotes character, shows intelligence. The skull is well developed, with a clearly-defined stop, and the muzzle lean, long, and square, with a powerful jaw. Eyes should be dark hazel, not light coloured. Liver and white, black and white or with tan markings is preferred. Coat straight, close and weather resisting without being coarse.

Welsh Springer Spaniels

THERE are a number of references to Spaniels in the ancient records of Wales. One of the first known mentions of these dogs appears in *The Laws of Howel Dda*, ruler of south Wales at the commencement of the tenth century. There it is stated that 'There are three higher species of dog: a tracker, a greyhound and a spaniel'. The spaniel of a king or of a man of high rank, say the old Laws, is valued at a pound. This was equal value to a stallion or the king's buckhound.

There is no suggestion that the Welsh Springers of today descend in a direct and unsullied line from those known to the law givers of Howel Dda, but up to the nineteenth century there were undoubtedly many varieties of dog whose strains had been kept pure for long periods of time. This was usually due either to the inaccessibility of the area or because they were exclusively owned by one family.

With the interest in dogs that arose in the nineteenth century, the increasing popularity of dog shows and the organisation of Field Trials, together with increasing ease and speed of travel the whole picture changed. Many types of dog were jostling for recognition as breeds and a number of doubtful claims to antiquity and sang pur were put forward. The Spaniel family was particularly difficult to sort out and the Spaniel Club undoubtedly did a great deal of excellent work, but in the case of the Springer Spaniels—whom they wished to call Norfolk Spaniels—there was much dissent and eventually they deleted the type entirely.

At that time show or 'fancier's' points had ruined many Spaniels for working purposes and there was an increasing feeling that these dogs should be able to do the work for which they were intended. The Sporting Spaniel Society had been founded to further this objective.

When Mr A. T. Williams' team of 'Welsh Spaniels' competed at the trials held at Tris-y-Gerwn and won in two successive years it aroused a considerable interest in the breed.

At Birmingham in 1899 the same Mr Williams had caused something of a sensation by winning the class for 'working type spaniels' with a dog called 'Corrin'. A great deal was said and written about 'Corrin', who soon became 'Ch. Corrin' and his breeder, Colonel Blandy Jenkins, claimed that his family and others in the neighbourhood of Neath had bred such red and white Spaniels for 'upwards of a hundred years' while Mr Williams believed the type to be 'probably the oldest of all the Spaniel breeds now in Britain'. It was largely due to this incident that, in 1902, the Kennel Club granted the Springers a place in their registers and sub-divided the breed into the English and Welsh varieties, despite the fact that many people felt that the Welshmen were nearer to the Cocker Spaniels.

For several years Mr Williams continued to be the breed's chief supporter and before long he was joined in the show ring by Mrs Green with her 'Longmynd' dogs. By 1913 Mr Williams had retired from both the show and Field Trial world and it looked as if the breed was declining. However, 1921 saw the breed succeeding in the field once more as Dr G. P. Barff was winning with 'Bacchus' and Colonel Downes Powell was scoring with his 'O'Matherne' dogs. At the present time several spaniel enthusiasts have taken up the breed and it seems to be in considerable demand.

DESCRIPTION OF THE WELSH SPRINGER

Not quite as big as English Springers. It will be seen that the ears are not as long: they narrow gradually towards the tip and are covered with feather that does not extend beyond the actual ear. They are placed moderately low and hang close to the cheek. The skull is fairly long and broad, with a stop below the eyes, and slightly rounded at the peak. The jaws, of medium length, are fairly square, a chubby head being disliked. Eyes hazel or dark. The length of body should be in proportion to the length of leg (medium); ribs deep and fairly well sprung; shoulders long and sloping; loin muscular and strong and slightly arched. Hindquarters strong, hocks well let down, stifles moderately bent. No feathering below hocks. Neck strong, muscular and clean in throat. Coat straight or flat, and thick. Colour dark rich red and white. Weight 35 to 45 lb.

Sussex Spaniels

THE history of Sussex Spaniels is fairly well authenticated. Mr Fuller of Rosehill Park, Brightling, was a keen shooting man who was interested in the breeding and work of the strain of spaniels which he had kept for fifty years. Mr Fuller died in 1847, so if he had had his dogs for half a century they were working in the eighteenth century. Since they claimed to descend from dogs owned by Mr Moneypenny of Rolvedon their history can be traced back to the time of George III or even earlier. On the death of Mr Fuller the kennel was dispersed, but Mrs Fuller allowed Relph, the head keeper, to keep the pair of Spaniels he preferred. These were 'George' and 'Romp' and one can presume that it is their portraits that illustrate Mr J. H. Walsh's description of the breed in his book *The Dog in Health and Disease*. Mr Relph, who outlived his master by forty years, retained a keen interest in these spaniels for the rest of his life. Mr Campbell Newington acquired some of the descendants of 'George' and 'Romp' and took 'Rosehill' as his kennel name. He bred and exhibited extensively, although at one period his kennel was almost depopulated by 'dumb madness', which is a name for rabies. It was probably the subsequent shortness of good stock that led to the infusion of black spaniel blood that took place about this time.

It was in the last five or six years of the last century that Mr Moses Woolland began to breed Sussex Spaniels and was determined to have the best of their kind. When his first two exhibits failed to win a prize he promptly bought the bitch that did, although she had an indifferent breeding reputation. From her and a dog called 'Battle', also purchased at a reasonable price, sprang a first-class line that included 'Bridford Bredaboy', 'Giddie', 'Daisy', 'Dolly' and 'Queenie'. While Mr Woolland concentrated entirely on the show ring Mr Campbell Newington both worked and exhibited the dogs from his kennel. Mr R. Chapman whose prefix 'Heather' has more recently been attached to Scottish Terriers owned 'Heather Glen' and 'May' and several other successful dogs.

The peculiarities of the true Sussex Spaniel are its colour and the fact that it can seldom be trained to hunt mute. This habit of babbling was considered by some to be a virtue and Mr J. H. Walsh remarks: 'He is gifted with a full, bell-like tongue which he varies according to the game before him, and by this means an experienced shooter can tell whether to expect "fur" or "feather" and can distinguish a hot scent from a stale one'. In more recent times a Spaniel who could not or would not hold his tongue would be considered anathema. The colour of the Sussex Spaniel should not be the usual deep liver or 'puce' shade common in other Spaniels, but a rich, golden-liver more like milk chocolate, although there is a golden glint when the light shines on the coat.

Since 1905 when the Bridford kennel was broken up the breed has found fewer and fewer supporters and at the present time the number of dogs and owners is very small and only the largest shows provide classes. A pity, since the Sussex is a pleasant and honest dog and it will be sad if he becomes extinct.

74

DESCRIPTION OF THE SUSSEX SPANIEL

Its distinctive colour should always be rich golden-liver. It is a heavyish dog, weighing from 40 to 50 lb. The skull is moderately long and also wide, with an indentation on the middle and a decided stop. Brows fairly heavy; occiput full, but not pointed. Eyes of hazel colour and fairly large, muzzle fairly long and square, and lips somewhat pendulous. Nostrils well-developed and a liver colour. Ears thick, fairly large, and lobe-shaped, set moderately low, carried close to the head and furnished with soft, wavy hair. Neck long, strong and slightly arched. There should not be much throatiness, but a well-marked frill in the coat. Shoulders sloping, chest deep and well-developed. Back and loin long and should be very muscular. The whole body is low, long, level and strong. Arms of the forelegs, and the thighs must be bony as well as muscular. Pasterns very short and bony. Feet large and round. Legs rather short and strong with great bone and moderately well feathered. The tail is docked from 5 to 7 in., set low and not carried above the level of the back, thickly clothed with moderately long feather. Body coat abundant, flat, with no tendency to curl.

Weimaraners

W E know very little about the ancestry of the Weimaraner and such knowledge as we have comes mainly from the United States rather than from Germany. In fact *German Dogs in Word and Picture*, published in Germany in 1928, does not mention the breed although it is fulsome in its praise of other German working dogs such as the Short-haired Pointer and the Pointing Griffon.

It is usually accepted that the Weimar Pointer came into existence somewhere in the first quarter of the seventeenth century and was exclusively owned by the Dukes of Weimar and a favoured few around his court. How the strange slate-blue colouring and light-coloured eyes came into the breed has never been satisfactorily explained. One suggestion being that they were brought about by faulty pigmentation caused by excessive in-breeding over a considerable period of time. The basic breeds involved were almost certainly the Pointer and, possibly, the Schweisshund, a type described as a bastard Bloodhound much esteemed for the excellence of its nose. Beyond the fact that these dogs are said to have been carefully bred at the court of Weimar where great emphasis was placed on their scenting ability, speed and courage, there is little more we know about their early history. Before the last war there appears to have been a club or clique interested in these dogs and whose rules, like those of many German breed societies, organised the members and their dogs with typical Germanic thoroughness. The dogs and their pedigrees were inspected by an official of the club and instructions issued as to which dog each bitch should be mated too; six puppies were the maximum number to be reared in any litter and these had to be registered. No exporting was allowed and all purchasers of puppies had to join the club. Quite a closed shop, in fact! In 1929 an American, Mr Howard Knight, became a member of the club and was eventually allowed to take two specimens of the breed back to the United States, where he founded an American club and endeavoured to run it on the same lines as the German.

The end of the last war widened the breed's horizons considerably. American troops and others who were occupying Germany saw these strange 'grey ghosts', while the hard conditions of the time broke down the club barriers. A number of the best dogs sailed to the States, where the breed made a considerable reputation for itself at obedience competitions.

In 1953 Weimaraners were first seen at Cruft's, most of them being dogs that had been imported to this country from the U.S.A. These dogs met with a mixed reception but six years later they had aroused enough interest for twenty-five of them to be registered and this number increased to seventy in the following year. Not a vast number in comparison to some breeds but enough to encourage English breeders who, in the short while they have been at work on these dogs, have done much to improve their soundness. The wobbling hocks, loose shoulders and nobby knee joints as well as weak pasterns of the early exhibits are fast disappearing.

In character the Weimaraner is a nice, friendly and rather clownish fellow whose unfamiliar pale amber or grey eyes make it hard for us to interpret his moods.

DESCRIPTION OF THE WEIMARANER

A medium-sized, short-coated dog, 23 to 25 in. high with a silver or mouse-grey coloured coat. Long aristocratic head with moderate stop. Long lobular ears set high. Eyes light amber, grey or blue-grey and set well apart. Nose grey. Strong body with back of moderate length, sloping slightly from the withers. Well-developed chest and well-sprung ribs and deep brisket. Forelegs straight and strong and the hindquarters are well angulated. Feet firm and compact with well-arched webbed toes and thick pads. The tail is docked so that it measures about 6 in. when the dog is fully grown.

TOY DOGS

WOMEN have always been attracted by something small, dainty and rare—if it should be alive, affectionate and confiding, how much greater the charm. The fourteen varieties of tiny or toy dogs that are familiar at the present time have come to us in different ways from a number of different countries—the Pekingese, the Pug and the Japanese from the Imperial Courts of China and Japan. The Maltese, once loved by the ladies of Greece and Rome, almost certainly originated in the island after which it is named, although no one knows how or why it evolved. Others, like the Italian Greyhound and those that are of Spaniel origin, are pygmyised editions of larger breeds. Here again the means by which the dwarfing was brought about are mysterious and various. Some seem to have been natural, while others were not. Mutations, glandular irregularities combined with selective breeding can be called natural but the dosing of puppies with strange infusions of herbs and daisy roots have all been recorded, while the Japanese dosed their little dogs with saki to stunt their growth. These methods are certainly not natural and those dogs who survived the treatment would produce young of a more normal size; nevertheless it may partly explain why the earliest Japanese bred in this country were larger than those preferred in their native land.

Man, however, can only claim to have improved on nature by selective breeding in his dealings with the dogs with short noses and wide muzzles; such breeds are basically or much crossed with *brachycephalic* canine types whose skull and jaw formations, from time immemorial, have differed from those of the long-headed *dolichocephalic* type.

Pygmyisation inevitably brings about certain physical characteristics—a shortening of the limbs, rounded or 'apple' heads and protruding or 'pop' eyes. Many of these characteristics can be seen in most of our toy breeds, although time and selective breeding have blended them into the proportions of the dog.

The tiny dogs of early times were not entirely without a purpose in life. Dame Juliana Berners in *The Boke of St Albans* (1486) refers to 'smale ladis popis that beere away the flees' or, in other words the fleas preferred a canine to a human host! Furthermore, there was a widely spread belief that if a small dog or 'comforter' was laid on the site of a sick person's pain the ill would travel from the human being to the dog. There are many references to this belief in a number of early writings and the term 'Comforter' was in common use as a description of a small dog over a long period of time. Curiously enough this same power of pain transference seems to have been attributed to the Xolocuintle or Hairless Dogs of Mexico up to quite recently.

Cosmopolitan in background, varied in appearance and character, the toy dogs are an extremely popular group of breeds and individuals fit in as well with the small home and busy life of the modern woman as they did with the leisured existence lived in the palaces and mansions of the past.

79

Chihuahuas

THERE is no breed more surrounded with fables and phantasies than the Chihuahua. Some of the stories may contain a grain or two of truth.

There are few people today who have not seen at least one tiny Chihuahua and know that the tale that they are hairless is not true. This story probably arose from confusion with another Mexican breed, the Xolocuintle, who has a skin like an elephant except for a few scrubby hairs on his forehead and tail.

During the 1920s and even earlier a few Chihuahuas arrived in this country but not many people saw them. So the legend arose that not only were they hairless, but that in their native country they lived in holes in the ground, climbing trees to hunt for food! One can only assume that the habit of allowing a Chihuahua to have far longer than usual nails on its rather prehensile but otherwise dainty feet gave rise to the tree climbing idea.

The lack of much knowledge about the history, religion and customs of the Aztecs has provided fertile ground for several unproveable tales about them and their dogs. It is said that the royal and noble Aztecs maintained huge numbers of tiny dogs who bore some resemblance to those we know today. One princess is believed to have maintained 1,500. Each dog in these noble establishments had its own slave to supply its needs, which included a diet of minced human infant. At the death of the dog the slave was killed and buried with it.

If little is known of Aztec customs, still less is known of their religion; but it does seem probable that their little dogs had some significance as guides to the spirits of the dead on their journey to the next world.

William Hickling Prescott in his *History of the Conquest of Mexico* has something to say about the birds and animals of Montezuma's menagerie, but makes no mention of dogs. In fact, almost all the archaeological evidence of dogs in the region of Mexico ante-dates the Aztec period and is derived from knowledge of the Toltec tribes. These people appear to have possessed small, but not tiny, heavily-boned mute dogs who served as hunting dogs as well as for food. It is possible, although there is no proof, that on the arrival of the Aztecs, who might have brought their hairless dogs with them, they and the Toltec dogs inter-bred and produced a line of small, round-eyed, bat-eared dogs that became popular as pets of the nobility and as food with the less privileged.

The likeness between the long-haired Chihuahua of today and the Papillon has often given rise to the question of whether the Spaniards carried dogs from the Old World to the New, or vice versa, but in view of the many Papillon-like dogs seen in European paintings of an earlier date than that on which Columbus returned to Spain, this is unlikely.

About 1850 another chapter opens. The peons of the Mexican province of Chihuahua began to sell tiny dogs to American tourists who came to see the ruins of Casas Grande, said to have been a palace of Montezuma. The little creatures were seldom old enough to leave their mothers and the majority died within a short time, but the survivors aroused an interest in both the United States and in Mexico. From these the modern breed was developed.

The British Chihuahua Club was formed in 1949; in 1954 the breed was granted championship status and 145 dogs were registered in this country. In 1961 the number was 1,978. There can be little doubt that the breed has come here to stay.

DESCRIPTION OF THE CHIHUAHUA

Average Chihuahua weights in this country are from 4 to 6 lb., but there are a few here weighing only 2½ lb. Chihuahuas are distinctive in appearance; their chief features being an apple domed head with deep stop, short pointed muzzle, full luminous eyes and large ears flaring out at the sides at an angle. Their bodies are compact, the length being slightly more than the height at the shoulders. The tail is of medium length carried up or over the back. Any colour or mixture of colours is permissible.

English Toy Terriers

UNTIL quite recently the official title of the English Toy Terrier (Black-and-Tan) was Black-and-Tan Terrier and before that simply the Toy Terrier. Until the arrival of the Chihuahua the breed had a good claim to produce some of the smallest specimens of the Toy breeds. The official standard puts the top permissible weight at 8 lb., but at a show a dog of such size would stand no chance whatsoever of winning the judge's favour.

The aim of the original breeders of these little dogs was to produce a perfect miniature Manchester Terrier. In the breed's standard of points the paragraph headed 'General Appearance' demands 'A Terrier calculated to take his own part in the rat pit, not of the Whippet type'. The Toy Terriers that were being produced a few years after fanciers got busy on reducing the Manchester Terrier would have been scared of a mouse!

The whole project was rather ill-timed and those who took part in it seem to have had no idea of even elementary genetics or selective breeding. Something was known of the subjects even in 1870. The Manchester Terriers with all the points the fanciers required were hard enough to breed and had already mislaid quite a lot of their sporting instincts as well as being subject to skin troubles and other minor ills. If breeders had concentrated first on producing a good healthy type of normal-sized Manchester Terriers before trying to produce miniatures they would have done much better. Instead they did everything possible that was wrong. It has always been believed that intense in-breeding results in the reduction of size—this doubtful policy might have met with some success if it had been carried out with sound and healthy specimens, but when the majority of the stock utilised were sickly or rickety it needs no knowledge of genetics to guess the outcome. To the usual problems of pygmyisation, such as pop-eyes, large round 'apple' heads and shortened limb bones, were added a general lack of resistance to disease and cold. The mortality rate was very high and most commentators of the period were critical of the dogs they saw around them. The crossing of the Toy Terrier with the Italian Greyhound did little good except to add the Italian's typical high stepping action to that of the terrier, thereby producing another fault. Undoubtedly there were a few good dogs in those days, but they were almost invariably bred from Manchester Terriers of small size. 'Sapolette' born in 1878 was, if pictures are to be believed, an excellent miniature Manchester Terrier who weighed about 5 lb. and she had the required flat-skulled head and perfect markings.

For years the breed gave up any pretensions of being anything but fancier's dogs, since its delicacy made it quite impossible for it to lead a normal dog's life. However, in the last few years there has been a genuine and apparently successful attempt to get back to the original objective and produce a miniature terrier with the correct appearance and characteristics. With the result that there is a greatly increased interest being taken in the breed by those who want a small pet and the number of registrations and show entries have risen quite considerably.

DESCRIPTION OF THE ENGLISH TOY TERRIER

The English Toy Terrier (Black-and-Tan) is a dwarf edition of the bigger Terrier, which is once more to be known by its former name of Manchester. The small ones should resemble the bigger in every respect, except for size. It is seldom, however, that the correct-shaped head is obtained to perfection in dwarfs: it should be long, flat and narrow, well filled up under the eyes, with tapering jaws. Lips tight, eyes very small, sparkling, dark, oblong in shape and set fairly closely together. An erect or semi-erect carriage of the ear is desirable. The neck should be fairly long and tapering from shoulders to head. Shoulders sloping and neck without throatiness. Body moderately short with an upward curve at the loins. Legs should be quite straight and fair of length, and the feet small and rounded. A tapering tail of moderate length, carried low. The smooth, short and glossy coat is easily groomed. Colour jet black and rich mahogany tan; the tan being distributed according to a well-recognised pattern. Weight should not exceed 8 lb.

Griffons Bruxellois

AS is the case with several breeds, opinions vary as to their origin. There are certainly a number of questions one can ask about the Griffon Bruxellois and his forefathers. That the breed originally came to this country from Belgium is certain. Undoubtedly a small, rough-coated dog with terrier characteristics seems to have been running around the Low Countries for several centuries. The term 'Griffon' simply means hairy or rough coated and has been applied to several Continental varieties of dog.

Many people are familiar with Jan van Eyck's painting 'The Marriage of Giovanni Arnolfini' painted about 1434 which hangs in the National Gallery. The little dog in the foreground has often been claimed as the ancestor of the modern Griffon Bruxellois. Other breeds have also claimed this little dog as one of their forefathers, but that put forward by the Griffon Bruxellois seems to be the most likely.

During the nineteenth century the cab drivers of several Belgian cities, especially those of Brussels, were in the habit of driving around with rough-coated terrier-like little dogs on their boxes: the little creatures yapped defiance at each other as their vehicles passed and then returned to the stables at night to deal with the mice and rats that rustled around in the straw. A few years later one or two dogs of this variety appeared at the early Continental dog shows held by the St Hubert Society. At first they shared their classes with another small and rather similar breed not often seen in this country— the Affenpinscher, but by 1886 they had classes to themselves and it was not long before a breed society was formed and the little Griffon dogs taken in hand quite drastically. At this time drastic changes took place in its make and shape, but quite what happened no one knows, although it is no secret that the Pug, the Affenpinscher and Toy Spaniels had a share in it, the result being an improvement in the eyes, expressions, fronts and coats of the Griffons, while reducing their size and length of nose.

At least one Griffon Bruxellois had been seen in this country about 1880, but about 1890 the breed began to attract serious attention. The first importations of any merit were 'Fox' and 'Bijou' who came from the kennels of the Duke of Flanders and Princess Helène. In 1898 the Griffons Bruxellois Club was founded. The first British champions were 'Bruno' and 'Mousquetaire Rouge'; Miss Wimbush owned the former and Mrs Moseley the latter. By this time Lady Handley Spicer's 'Copthorne', Miss Hall's 'Park Place' and Mrs Howarth's kennels had been formed, and so many dogs were being imported from Belgium that some anxiety was aroused in case the parent country should lose all its best stock.

At the present time the Griffons Bruxellois in this country have survived the difficulties of two wars and the breed is in the very happy position of being reasonably but not excessively popular. The rough-coated dogs are often known as Griffons Bruxellois while the smooth-coated variety—who are the most nearly related to the Pugs—are called Petit Brabancon. The black and black-and-tan varieties are Griffons Belges, but all three types are inter-bred and each coat and colour as welcome as the other when they appear in the same litter.

In character the Griffons have many quaint and endearing habits and their monkey faces have enormous charm. They have no wish to be pampered lap dogs since they are sound and stocky with the courage and heart of a lion.

DESCRIPTION OF THE GRIFFON BRUXELLOIS

The head is noticeable because it is large and rounded, covered with rather coarse hair and the jaws edged with moustache and beard. Ears small and semi-erect; in imported specimens they may be cropped and upright. The chest is rather wide and deep; legs of medium length, and the tail, which is carried upwards, is, roughly, two-thirds docked. Medium ones are the most valued, though the weight may range between 3 and 10 lb. Colour red or black or black and rich tan. In Belgium the black is known as the Griffon Belge. There is a smooth-coated variety which is useful for breeding with the roughs. These are called Brabançons, the word 'Griffons' not being applicable, as it simply means rough.

Italian Greyhounds

I TALY has no true proprietary rights in the miniature Greyhounds who have taken Italian nationality, although many good ones are still bred in that country. These little dogs have been scattered widely over Europe since the fourteenth century and our knowledge of them is largely gleaned from their appearance in the works of the great masters of painting: Jan van Eyck, Memling, Veronese and Watteau, to mention but a few.

Charles I is said to have been the first Italian Greyhound owner in this country, but this overlooks the fact that his mother, Anne of Denmark, was painted by Paul van Somer with five small, but not tiny, Greyhounds around her feet. Charles I did, however, have a tiny Greyhound as his constant companion and one accompanied him to his execution. Throughout their history Italian Greyhounds have been the property of royalty and nobility and something inherited from this environment is conveyed by their soignée appearance and assured manners. Among their royal owners have been Catherine the Great, Frederick the Great and Queen Victoria.

In eighteenth-century books dealing with dogs we find frequent references to Italian Greyhounds. Thomas Bewick considered them 'exquisitely beautiful and delicate'; gruff old Taplin thought them 'dedicated only to the comforts of the tea table', while some years later J. H. Walsh ('Stonehenge') describes them as 'one of the most beautifully proportioned animals in creation'.

It was, however, around the period of 'Stonehenge' that the deterioration of the English dogs of the breed set in, largely owing to the habit of in-breeding to an excessive and ridiculous degree. Among the winners at the earliest shows were 'Silvey' and the dove-coloured 'Molly', the latter said to be the finest of her kind yet seen.

By the end of the last century the stupid in-breeding programme that had been practised, together with the desire for diminutiveness that had led to crosses with toy terriers, brought disaster. Sterility, lack of stamina and intelligence, together with pop eyes and apple heads, became prevalent. For some years the breed lost favour. It was, however, too charming to be eclipsed for long and early in the present century determined and successful efforts were made to improve the breed. Sir Walter Shelley and Miss Mackenzie worked hard on behalf of the little Greyhounds and the latter's bitch 'Ch. Hero' gained many successes. The breed had become very popular in the United States and its future looked bright, but by some quirk of fashion a decline set in once more.

Numbers fluctuated during the years that followed, but by 1952 it seemed quite possible that the Italian Greyhound might die out entirely in this country, for only five were registered. This was the nadir of the breed. Shocked by the state of affairs, the few remaining breeders made heroic efforts, and numbers began to rise once more and badly needed new blood was imported. 'Ulisse di Peltrengo', bred in Italy and imported by Mrs Mooney, was a wonderful advertisement for the breed and he soon became the first Italian-bred dog to become an English champion. He made his presence felt as a sire and, when he himself was re-sold to America, he left some excellent stock behind him.

The popularity of a charming breed has been handicapped by the belief that it is delicate and needs coddling. In fact it needs no more than good dry quarters, suitable food and the reciprocation of its own affection.

86

DESCRIPTION OF THE ITALIAN GREYHOUND

In appearance it is a miniature Greyhound and has all the grace and shape, symmetry and action of that breed. In movement the Italian Greyhound is high stepping with a free and graceful action. The head is finely moulded, the large bright eyes dark and full of expression and the small rose-shaped ears are soft and delicate. The neck is long and curved, the back is arched and ends in a fine long tail. The coat is thin and glossy, the skin fine and supple. The colour of the coat varies from fawn, white, cream, blue, black, and fawn and white pied. The weight of a fully grown dog should not exceed 10 lb. and 6 to 8 lb. is the ideal.

Japanese

THE little dogs known to the Japanese as 'chin' lived in the land of almond blossom and Fujiyama for many centuries, but there is a strong suspicion that China may well have been the land of their origin. The Pekingese and the Japanese dog have certain outward similarities, although they are poles apart in character. Dogs of one sort or another have so often been royal gifts that there is nothing in the least impossible in the suggestion that some of the little dogs favoured by the Emperors of China carried his compliments to the court of the Mikado. When or how we do not know, but those with a knowledge of the Japanese language have said that the name 'chin', used for the Japanese dogs, is written by a character that has an affinity with the one meaning 'Chinese' and 'dogs'.

These little dogs were looked on as precious toys in the royal and noble households of Japan, where they were carefully bred and carefully fed—mainly on rice. The puppies were often given saki in order to stunt their growth since the smaller the dog the more it was valued.

It is known that there was frequent trade between East and West from the fourteenth century, but there is no record of any of the Japanese dogs coming to this country until just before 1862 and no details are known of those that arrived then except that they are said to have appeared at an English dog show in that year. We hear them mentioned again in 1873 and as 'Japanese Pugs' in 1879—a name that was afterwards altered to Japanese Toy Spaniels. It is clear, however, that the Japanese dogs arrived in this country earlier than their relations the Pekingese. 'Ming Seng', owned by Mr Marples, was probably the first typical, even if rather large, Japanese to attract any serious attention. It was about this time that the Mikado sent the Empress of Germany a pair of Japanese and the fame of the breed began to spread over Europe. A few years later the Princess of Wales, later Queen Alexandra, became enamoured of these dainty little dogs and whenever possible a number of these dogs kept her company.

The early importations to this country were quite naturally the pets of people who had lived in, or visited, Japan, but with increasing popularity efforts were made to find good dogs in their native land to improve the breed in this country. Unfortunately the old days of careful breeding had passed and Japanese dogs were only too often either big and coarse or small and weedy. Therefore, it was largely left to British breeders to do their best with what stock they had already got.

The Pekingese is aloof and resentful of strangers who press their attentions upon him and bestows his friendship on a carefully selected few—the Japanese is gay and merry and only too willing to offer his affection to all and sundry. His appearance has been likened to a butterfly as well as to a chrysanthemum—both are apt comparisons in view of his dainty, feathery coat, plumy tail and the typical head and ear markings.

DESCRIPTION OF THE JAPANESE

These dogs should be essentially stylish in movement, lifting the feet high when in motion, carrying the tail (which is heavily feathered) proudly, curved or plumed over the back. The head should be large for the size of the dog, with a broad skull, rounded in front; the muzzle is very short, the upper lips being rounded on each side of the nostrils, which should be large and black except in the case of red and white dogs, in which brown-colour red noses are as common as black ones. The eyes should be large, dark, and set far apart, and it is desirable that the white shows in the inner corners which gives to this breed the characteristic look of astonishment. The ears should be small, set wide apart, and high on the dog's head; carried slightly forward and V-shaped. The legs should be straight and the bone fine, well feathered to the feet. The body should be squarely and compactly built, wide in chest and 'cobby' in shape. The length of the body should roughly be equal to its height. The coat should be long, profuse, and straight, free from curl or wave and not too flat. It should have a tendency to stand out, more particularly at the frill, with profuse feathering on the tail and thighs. As regards colour, the dog should be either Black and White or Red and White, i.e. parti-colour. The term red includes all shades of sable, brindle, lemon and orange. The white should be clear and the colour, whether black or red, evenly distributed as patches over the body, cheek and ears.

King Charles Spaniels

IT has often been suggested, but it has never been proved, that spaniels first came to this country from Spain. It does, however, seem extremely likely that some of the earliest 'toy spaniels' may have come to this country as gifts of Philip of Spain to his wife Mary, Queen of England. The portrait of the Queen and her husband at Woburn Abbey shows them accompanied by two small white dogs of a spaniel type. This may be an inspired guess, but this type of dog was certainly popular as royal pets at the period and it is well known that Mary, Queen of Scots owned a little spaniel who crept beneath her skirts at the moment of her execution.

By the time Charles II was seated on the throne the palaces of England were full of Spaniels and their royal master allowed them not only the freedom of his apartments but also of the council chambers. Pepys made several sour remarks about the royal dogs and, when describing a meeting of the Privy Council, he writes 'all I observed was the silliness of the King, playing with his dogs all the while, and not minding the business'.

For a number of years after the House of Stuart had made way for the House of Orange not much is heard of pet Spaniels, although John Churchill, first Duke of Marlborough, favoured a small, but not tiny, sporting variety which became known as Blenheim Spaniels and could still be seen around Woodstock in 1880.

In the last century toy spaniels slowly came into the limelight once more. The breeding of them in back rooms and cellars to supply parlour pets for the Victorian ladies became quite an industry. The general appearance of these dogs had changed a great deal in the years that intervened between the time of the Stuarts and the days of the Victorians. Short, flat faces and plenty of feathering had become desirable features. The flat faces may well have come about through an association with Pugs, whose popularity had increased as that of the toy spaniel decreased.

English toy spaniels, under the headings of Blenheim Spaniels and King Charles Spaniels, were exhibited from the earliest days of organised dog shows, but owing to the habit of duplicating names it is difficult to know which dogs had an influence on their breeds. In 1885 the Toy Spaniel Club was founded and in 1892 the breed was classified in the Kennel Club Stud Book.

Although the various colours are now generally inter-bred and classed together as King Charles Spaniels, the whole coloured reds are known as 'Rubies'; 'Blenheims' are white with chestnut red patches. The tri-colours were once known as Prince Charles Spaniels, but this title is now not much used; here the white ground colouring is patched with black, with tan markings on the cheeks, over the eyes, inside the ears and under the tail. The black-and-tan colouring was once the most favoured variety and the earliest to be called 'King Charles', as opposed to the general title of 'toy spaniels' and the ground colour is black with tan markings disposed as on the tri-colours.

The King Charles Spaniel is a charming small dog, intelligent and affectionate. When young he is reasonably active, but in later life he becomes rather addicted to comfort.

DESCRIPTION OF THE KING CHARLES SPANIEL

In shape they are compact and cobby; wide and deep in chest; low to ground. Best size from 6 to 12 lb. Skull massive; well domed, and full over the eyes. Nose very short and turned up to meet the skull. Deep stop; cheeks well cushioned; ears very long, well feathered and set low. Eyes dark and large, and set wide apart. Coat long, silky, and straight with profuse feathering on the usual parts. The Black-and-Tan variety should be a rich, glossy black, with bright mahogany tan markings. The tricolour has a ground of pearly white, with well distributed black patches and brilliant tan markings; wide white blaze between the eyes and up the forehead. Blenheim on a ground of pearly white, chestnut red patches; a white blaze with a red mark in the centre of the skull. Ruby, whole colour, rich chestnut red.

Cavalier King Charles Spaniels

EVEN before 1926 it had often been remarked that the King Charles Spaniels of the show bench and the drawing-room bore little resemblance to the little Spaniels seen in so many notable paintings of the Stuart period and who were so often mentioned by writers of the seventeenth century. The Spaniels loved by Charles II seem, like their royal master, to have been merry dogs. The little animals scampered about the palaces and appeared both on state occasions and at meetings of the Privy Council. The arrival of the House of Orange demoted the Spaniels from their position and the Pugs took their place as court favourites. The popularity and undoubted charm of the Pug, with his short nose and large eyes, may have been responsible for the idea that the 'toy spaniel' would be improved by a change in its features; maybe an accidental alliance started the whole thing, but no one knows.

In 1926 the lovers of King Charles Spaniels were startled, and some were shocked, by an announcement that appeared in the schedule of classes and prizes offered at the forthcoming Cruft's Show. Mr Roswell Eldridge, of New York, offered two first prizes of £25 'for Blenheim Spaniels of the old type as shown in pictures of Charles II's time: long face, no stop, flat skull not inclined to be domed, with spot in centre of the skull'— in fact, everything that the modern King Charles Spaniel was not. The suggested models were the dogs in the Landseer painting to be seen in the Tate Gallery. This was a little awkward since Landseer's Spaniels had definite 'stops', although their noses were far longer than the current fashion.

At Cruft's that year only two Spaniels competed for the £25, but, despite some dissension among breeders, a seed had been sown on fertile ground, where it slowly germinated. Previously any puppy showing signs of having a flat skull or even a rudimentary nose had been considered of no value, but now they became in great demand by those interested in this change of type and who took the dogs in the old Dutch pictures as their models. Mrs Raymond Mallock who had owned many toy breeds added this new type to her kennels and her dog 'Anne's Son' bore a striking likeness to the dogs painted by van Dyck; in consequence he became the ancestor of many modern 'Cavaliers'. 'Hentzau Love Lily' and 'Hentzau Sweet Nell' both won the £25 during the five years in which it was offered. Mrs Pitt, the owner of 'Sweet Nell', became the secretary of the Cavalier King Charles Spaniel Club.

Naturally things did not settle down all at once and quite a lot of selective breeding had to be done. Also, it is whispered, some Cocker Spaniel blood was added to the mixture, before the Cavalier bred true to anything like his present appearance.

Thus, a new breed carrying old blood was born and at the present time it is one of the most popular of 'toy' breeds' In actual fact there is nothing 'toy' about the Cavalier for he is lively and active with distinctly sporting instincts and a fondness for exercise. This is just as well, since like most Spaniels he is a good, hearty trencherman who is not fussy about the food that is placed in his dish.

DESCRIPTION OF THE CAVALIER KING CHARLES SPANIEL

The standard describes the Cavalier as a lively, active, fearless little dog of 10 to 18 lb. in weight. The head should be almost flat between the ears, without dome, the spot is desirable in Blenheim specimens; nose black, about 1½ in. in length, having a slight stop. The eyes should be dark, large and well placed apart. Muzzle pointed, and coat long and silky, all recognised colours, ears set high, long and well feathered, chest moderate; length of tail optional; moderate bone in legs, feet well feathered. An undershot jaw or light eyes are faults.

93

Maltese

THE Maltese is undoubtedly the oldest of all the toy varieties of dog. The dogs of Malta or *Canes Melitaei* attracted the attention of Strabo (born 64 B.C.), who wrote they 'are not bigger than common ferrets or weasels; yet they are not small in common understanding nor unstable in their love'. There are several other classical references that make it plain that dogs from Malta were the valued playthings of the ladies of both Greece and Rome.

When or how the little dogs from the Mediterranean island arrived in this country is not known—possibly the returning Crusaders may have brought them as presents for their ladies, but history offers no definite support for this suggestion. The dogs were, however, known by the time Dr Johannes Caius, physician to Queen Elizabeth I, wrote a famous treatise endeavouring to classify dogs into types and breeds for his friend in Switzerland, Dr. Gesner. Under the heading Spaniel Gentle or Comforters he writes: 'There is another sort of gentle dogges in our Englishe style . . . the dogges of this sort does Callimachus call Mellitaeis of the Island Melita'.

Another author refers to these small dogs as 'little and prettie, proper and fine'. References to these dogs as 'shock dogs' appear with some frequency through the ages. By the end of the eighteenth century pictures supplant words, for Sir Joshua Reynolds painted both Nellie O'Brian and Miss Emilia Vansittart accompanied by dogs that are easily recognisable as Maltese.

The nineteenth century changed the picture somewhat. Travellers brought home dogs from Malta, but those that survived both the journey and the change of climate were inferior to those already here, and often grew to a great size. The 'fanciers', so prevalent in the early days of dog showing, took a hand in the matter and brought over dogs from the Continent, where the breed had always been popular. There is also more than a suspicion that they made use of Poodles for improving the coat, although the Maltese has often been credited with helping to diminish the size of Poodles. Pedigrees were far from being holy writ in those days.

Maltese began their career at British dog shows in June, 1862, and the winner's name was simply 'Mick', while the second prize went to 'Fido', both owned by Mr R. Mandeville. Several importations are recorded around this period and at least two of them came, somewhat surprisingly, from Manilla.

The breed has never achieved great popularity and at the end of the last century it was soon outnumbered by Pugs, Pomeranians and later by Pekingese.

Although one expects a Maltese to be a white dog, and would be surprised if it were otherwise, any self-colour is acceptable according to the English standard of points.

By nature the Maltese is sweet tempered and intelligent and has quite a lot of terrier characteristics. Beneath his profusion of white and silky coat he is a soundly built little dog well capable of enjoying exercise and fun.

DESCRIPTION OF THE MALTESE

The most conspicuous feature of the Maltese is the long silky coat, not in any way woolly, but straight. Any self-colour is recognised, but it is desirable that they should be pure white. Slight lemon markings do not penalise. The head, of a terrier shape, should not be too long, too narrow or rounded in skull. Ears long and well feathered, hanging close to the head. Eyes dark brown with black rims and not too far apart. Nose black. Legs short and straight, feet round. Body short and cobby, low to ground, and back straight from top of shoulders to tail. Tail well arched over back and well feathered. Size from 4 to 9 lb., the smaller the better. They should have a sharp terrier appearance with lively action.

Miniature Pinschers

THERE have been several attempts to popularise Miniature Pinschers in this country, but each time circumstances prevented these smart, gay little Continental dogs from establishing themselves. Early in the 1950s a further effort was made and this seems to have met with success, for the breed was soon numerically large enough to have been granted championship status in 1958.

Miniature Pinschers—more familiarly known as 'Minpins'—have been an accepted Continental breed for two or three centuries so we are told, although no one has attempted to explain how or why they came about. A strange but interesting book issued by the German Kennel Club in 1928 to tell the English speaking peoples all about German breeds makes no mention of them. Undoubtedly the German Pinscher Club was formed in 1895 but later changed its title to the Pinscher-Schnauzer Klub. 'Pinscher' is a wide term employed in the titles of several Continental breeds and calls up a picture of a smart, sharp dog of terrier type; until very recently it was both usual and correct to refer to 'Dobermann Pinschers' but the affix is now dropped. Nevertheless there is a strong resemblance between the tiny 'Minpins' and the far larger Dobermanns. In its native land this miniature breed is often called the 'Reh Pinscher' owing to its likeness to a deer of that name.

Miniature Pinschers travelled to the United States long before they ever reached these islands, probably owing to quarantine laws and ear cropping difficulties. Without doubt American breeders did a great deal to improve the breed after its arrival there somewhere about 1919. It did not become really popular, however, until some ten years later when the Miniature Pinscher Club of America was formed.

Miniature Pinschers, most of them of Continental breeding, appeared at Cruft's and other shows in 1954, entered in classes for breeds not otherwise classified, and they certainly attracted quite a lot of attention. A number of successful exhibitors of other breeds became interested in a type of dog that they thought might soon be in great demand. A number of dogs were imported from the Continent and, somewhat later, from the United States.

When the breed achieved championship status in 1958 the value of the American blood immediately became clear. The breed's first champion 'Chaman Kaama of Tavey', born in 1956, was of American parentage; the bitch 'Chaman Minnehaha', who qualified in 1959, was almost equally of Continental and American descent. When these two were mated they produced the dog 'Ch. Chaman Pawnee' in 1957 and the bitch 'Ch. Chaman Beeswing' on 24th December, 1958. 'Beeswing' was an exceptionally find Christmas gift, for at the time of writing she has won fourteen Challenge Certificates and is the dam of 'Ch. Birling Blissful', who will probably outshine her mother. The breed has not yet justified the high hopes that were held for a tremendous rush of public interest, but perhaps it is early days yet to give up hope.

DESCRIPTION OF THE MINIATURE PINSCHER

The Miniature Pinscher is a vigorous compact little dog of elegant appearance. Height is from 10 to 12 in. There are various colours, the most popular being red or stag red and black and rust. The coat is naturally very glossy and requires little attention. The head must be proportionate to the body, tapering to a fairly strong muzzle. The back must be level and the tail well set and docked short. Legs must have strong and sound bone development. Movement resembles the true action of a hackney pony.

Papillons

TO express an opinion about the origin of the Papillon or Butterfly dog is to invite argument. Since space is limited it is possibly wiser to pass over the theory held by some, that the Papillon's ancestors travelled from the New World to Europe at the time of Christopher Columbus and Vespucci, and concentrate on the more likely belief that these little dogs are a branch of the large toy spaniel family known to have been popular playthings in many courts and palaces of Europe. Such little dogs have appeared in the paintings of many Italian, Florentine, Flemish, Dutch, French and English artists since the fourteenth century. It is notable, therefore, that Christopher Columbus did not return to Spain until the late fifteenth century.

To anyone interested in pictures these small Spaniels will be familiar—they are minor, but often useful, factors in a composition. They varied in colour, but all had little pointed faces, were small in size and, with one exception, they had large, drop ears.

Where, when or by whom selective breeding was first practised and a certain measure of standardisation of type achieved, one does not know. The writers of the last century are singularly silent on the subject. The Papillon breed gained its name from its large, heavily fringed and obliquely set ears that give an impression of a butterfly in flight. The ears are the outstanding physical characteristic of the breed and they may be carried erect or dropped—the former being the most usual. On the Continent dogs that carry their ears in the dropped position are often called Phalènes.

It is possible that there were one or two of these little dogs in this country at the beginning of the present century and they were definitely here in 1906. By that time there was a certain uniformity of style and type which had been achieved by Continental breeders, mainly in France and Belgium.

The major invasion of this country by Papillons started in 1923. In the United States the breed had been increasing in popularity since 1906 and the first American champion gained his title in 1915. In this country several Papillons appeared in the class for 'Foreign Dogs' at the 1923 Kennel Club Show. The breed aroused immediate enthusiasm and was granted championship status a year later. With the understandable exception of the war years, the Papillon has made steady progress—not to great heights of popularity but in type, stamina and temperament as well as in the affections of those that know them.

Papillons are dainty and gentle but not delicate. While they are extremely active and vivacious one can hardly expect to refer to a finely-boned atom, who weighs but a few pounds, as 'sporting'; but they are not lacking in courage or interest in people and possibilities.

DESCRIPTION OF THE PAPILLON

The Papillon's upright ears should be very big and heavily fringed and they are carried with the tips pointing outwards. In general appearance they are smart, lively and intelligent. They should not measure more than 12 in. at the shoulder, nor weigh over 9 lb., but the tinier they are the better, the ideal weight being between 3 and 6 lb. The head is small, with a slightly rounded skull and a fine pointed muzzle. Eyes round and placed rather low in the head, dark in colour.

Light noses are regarded as a fault, but not a disqualification. The back is straight and not too short. The chest rather deep, and the loins a trifle arched. The legs are straight, fine, and rather short, and the feet comparatively long. The long, fringed tail falls over the back like that of a squirrel. Coat long and silky. Colours white with black or coloured patches. Head markings should be symmetrical; the white blaze up to the face should be clearly defined.

Pekingese

WITH Pekingese, so deservedly popular with those that like their dogs to combine beauty and character, it is difficult to believe that the breed was almost unknown in the western hemisphere less than a hundred years ago or that they made their first appearance in the show ring as recently as 1894.

The early history of these dogs is too long and too involved to be gone into here. Let the story start with the dogs owned by the last of the great Imperial Chinese breeders —'Her Imperial Majesty T'su Hsi, Dowager Empress of the Flowery Land of Confucius'. The Dowager Empress, who disliked all Europeans and exhorted her dogs 'to bite all foreign devils instantly', was found dead by her own hand when the British and French troops sacked the Summer Palace at Pekin in 1860. Around her body were the five little dogs who were destined to travel to England and arouse such an interest in their breed that it was to become the most popular of all toy dogs.

Some say that more than five dogs were found that sadly historic day, but it is only of these three bitches and two dogs that we have any definite knowledge. One pair were given by Lord John Hay to the Duchess of Wellington, the second pair to the Duchess of Richmond and Gordon and a tiny fawn and white bitch, called by her captors 'Looty', was presented by Captain Dunne to Queen Victoria and lived a long and happy life at Windsor.

Strangely enough none of these dogs bred, but such was their charm that both the Duchess of Wellington and the Duchess of Richmond managed to acquire further dogs from China. From the Duchess of Richmond's dogs sprang the 'Goodwood' strain which was to become famous in the ownership of her sister-in-law, Lady Algernon Gordon-Lennox.

Importations became increasingly difficult during the next few years since for a Chinese to sell a dog to a foreigner was almost a crime. But Captain Loftus Allen sent 'Pekin Peter' to his wife in 1894, in which year this dog appeared and won a prize at Chester Show. In 1896 'Ah Cum' and 'Mimosa' were smuggled out of the country packed in a box of hay that accompanied some Japanese deer. The last exports from the Imperial kennels were 'Glanbrane Boxer' and 'Quaema' who were given to Major Gwynne by Prince Ch'ing in return for a safe conduct from the city at the time of the Boxer rising.

The enthusiasm for Pekingese grew rapidly in this country and it was not long before they displaced Pomeranians from their position as popular favourites. One of the famous breeders of the time was Mrs Ashton Cross whose 'Alderbourne' kennel is still carried on by her daughters. In the United States enthusiasm for Pekingese has always been as great as it is in this country and although many excellent dogs have been bred there many outstanding British-bred Pekes have crossed the Atlantic and added further honours to their list.

No one can deny the Pekingese his charm—dignified and calculating, he knows his own rights and worth. Obstinate to a degree, he can be infuriating but he is never disloyal. Usually completely fearless a 'Peke' makes a good house dog and a very intelligent companion. His infant sons and daughters are quite enchanting.

100

DESCRIPTION OF THE PEKINGESE

Pekingese are hardy, intelligent, and amusing, to say nothing of their beauty of coat and eccentricity of appearance. The shape is leonine, the body being comparatively heavy in front and tapering off to the waist. The head should be massive, too, the skull being wide and flat between the ears, which are long, drooping and well feathered. The wrinkled muzzle is very short and broad. Legs very short, the front ones being bowed out at elbows. Behind, they are lighter, but firm and well shaped. The coat is long, straight, and flat, not curly. Thick undercoat. Profuse feathering on thighs, legs, tail and toes. A heavy mane forms a frill round the front of the neck, and the curled tail is carried proudly over the loins. Colours are numerous and beautiful. The ideal weight is between 7 and 12 lb.

Pomeranians

THE Pomeranian of today is an effervescent ball of fluff with a bright and beady eye and a plumy tail. It was not always so.

The Pomeranians of earlier years were far larger dogs and perhaps the most typical of the 'Spitz' breeds. The 'Spitz' family have provided the world with many useful dogs including watch dogs, draught dogs and, in China, edible dogs. The family's most noticeable physical characteristics are upstanding ears, pointed faces, and tails that curl tightly over their backs.

Until about 1885 the Pomeranians in this country were almost exclusively white and weighed about 20 lb. and sometimes more. As their name implies the breed came to this country from the Continent and had connections with Pomerania. English writers of the nineteenth century do not appear to have liked these dogs over-much, describing them as surly tempered and snappish, and their reputation with children was bad. About 1886 the situation began to alter and Pomeranians of several colours, with blacks in the majority, began to appear in the show ring and eventually almost ousted the whites. Many of these dogs were imported from Germany, but as the breed became more and more fashionable, obviously more and more were bred in this country. Most contemporary writers were fair-minded enough to admit that these coloured and far smaller dogs had much nicer temperaments than their predecessors.

Part of the reason for the Pomeranian's rapid rise in public favour was undoubtedly the affection Queen Victoria evinced for the breed. Quite a number were housed in the royal kennels and others were royal house companions. 'Windsor Marco' is the dog of whom we know most. He weighed about 12 lb. and is described as being of a deep red sable colour with tail and hind featherings of 'a very pale tint of the same hue, almost white'. Marco and some of his kennel companions appeared at a number of dog shows where they not only won prizes but by the very fact of their appearance at such events they set a seal of respectability on the hobby of dog breeding and dog exhibiting. The dogs favoured by Queen Victoria usually weighed about 12 lb.—smaller than the earlier dogs but larger than those that were rapidly becoming fashionable, for classes for dogs 'not exceeding 8 lb. (Toys)' soon became usual. It was not long before the Toy Pomeranian became the great favourite and ousted Pugs from their premier position in both the show ring and the drawing room.

The rapidity with which size had been diminished together with the craze for colour breeding handicapped the progressive breeding of good Pomeranians and the breed was soon accused, with some truth, of lack of both stamina and brains. Its popularity inevitably began to decline and the Pekingese soon reigned in its place.

It is rare today to meet a Pomeranian in the street or in the parks. Nevertheless, the breed still exists. Beautiful, tiny dogs are seen at the shows, but they have become a specialist's breed, needing too much care and attention for the ordinary citizen to provide. Despite his present tiny size the Pom is no fool, but unfortunately he has never learnt to be seen and not heard.

DESCRIPTION OF THE POMERANIAN

The Pomeranian's head is foxy or wedge-shaped, surmounted by tiny erect ears. The neck and back are short, and the body well ribbed; straight, well-feathered forelegs of medium length, neither too long nor too short. The tail lies flat and straight over the back, and is profusely covered with long, harsh, spreading hair. The undercoat is soft and fluffy, and the outer long, perfectly straight and of harsh texture, forming an abundant frill round the neck. The hindquarters have long feathering. All the whole colours are admissible, but they should be perfectly sound and free from black or white shadings. The pure whites have rather gone out of fashion. There are also particoloured dogs, the colours of which are evenly distributed in patches.

Pugs

THE ancestry of the Pug has aroused considerable controversy at various times, but it is now generally agreed that the breed had its roots in China and has no relationship with the Mastiff. Mr V. W. F. Collier, the author of that scholarly book *The Dogs of China and Japan*, has no doubt about the origin of the Pug and says 'that the English Pug is descended from the Chinese dog may be considered as settled' and quotes many authorities to support his opinion.

Starting with the Han dynasty there has been almost continuous trade in silk and merchandise between China and the West and trade relations were opened with Portugal in 1516, with Spain in 1575, with the Dutch in 1604 and with England thirty-three years later. An overland trade route between China and Russia was opened at the time of Peter the Great. How probable that the sailors and travellers of that time returned from their journeys with small, strange little dogs that would please the ladies of Europe.

The story of the Pug or 'camus' who saved the life of William the Silent by giving the alarm when his camp was attacked by the Spanish is too well known and too long to quote in full. This incident, however, was responsible for William the Silent's devotion to the breed and this affection was carried down to his descendant, William of Orange who, when he and his wife Mary arrived in England in 1688, brought their dogs with them. Pugs, usually decked with bows of orange ribbon, became the favourite pets of the English court.

Pugs are mentioned with some frequency in the literature of the seventeenth and eighteenth centuries and a Pug dog was an almost essential part of a fashionable lady's accessories. George III was fond of Pugs but not so devoted as his wife, Charlotte of Mecklenberg, who kept and bred them in considerable numbers. Her dogs may possibly have had a considerable effect on the future development of the breed.

During the first fifty years of the last century two strains dominated the breed—that of Mr Morrison of Walham Green: his dogs were of a pale apricot fawn colour. Mr Morrison confided to Mr J. H. Walsh that his strain was founded on royal dogs— presumably the Pugs of the palace were smuggled down the back stairs to meet the Pugs of Walham Green. The second important strain was that owned by Lord and Lady Willoughby de Eresby. The foundations of this strain are uncertain for some say that Lord Willoughby de Eresby obtained a dog from the French tight-rope walker Charles Blondin; other authorities say it came from a Hungarian Countess. One of the most famous and important Pugs of all time was a dog called 'Click' owned by Mrs Mayhew. Click's parents 'Moss' and 'Lamb' were almost certainly imported from China.

The early part of the Victorian era was the hey-day of the Pug both as a show dog and as a drawing room pet, but all through Pug history its popularity has gone in cycles. The arrival of the Pekingese turned the wheel again and Pugs retired from the centre of the stage and have only recently returned.

The Pug, whether black or fawn, is a charming small dog if not allowed to get too fat. By nature he is active and merry, but unfortunately greedy, and it is when he loses his waistline that he also loses interest in anything but his own comfort.

DESCRIPTION OF THE PUG

The Pug is a compact dog, being square and cobby, and he has substance in little. The weight may vary from 14 to 18 lb. The short body is well ribbed up and is wide in chest. Legs strong, straight and of moderate length. The head is distinctive, being massive, round and with no indentation of the skull. The muzzle is short, blunt and square. Eyes prominent and dark in colour. The markings of the silvers and apricot-fawns should be clearly defined, with the mask, ears, mole on cheeks, thumb mark on forehead and trace as black as possible. Solid blacks are also frequently seen. The tail is curled tightly over the hip, a double curl being considered perfection. The coat is fine, smooth, soft and glossy.

Yorkshire Terriers

IT is mainly due to its diminutive size that the Yorkshire is classified among the toy breeds; if it were to be judged by its character it would certainly be among the terriers from whom it originally sprung.

The modern Yorkshire Terrier is a 'made up' breed and there is no secret about it. The Yorkshire weavers and artisans of the last century aimed at producing a small terrier who would not be too large for a life in their tiny cottages but would be game and sporting enough to deal with rats either in or out of a rat pit. The early objective was a dog weighing about 12 or 15 lb. The ingredients they used to produce their ideal are as mysterious as the contents of a sausage. A small local type of black-and-tan or blue-and-tan terrier seems to have been the root stock and probably crosses with Dandie Dinmont Terriers and Skye Terriers followed. Later, when long silky coats and smaller size became the fashion a dash of Maltese may well have been added to the mixture.

At the earliest shows at which these terrier types made an appearance they appear to have been entered in classes for 'Scotch Terriers', but by 1880 there were classes for 'Broken-haired or Yorkshire Terriers'. Three years later Mrs M. A. Foster's 'Bradford Hero' seems to have swept the board and the same owner's 'Huddersfield Ben' can be considered as the father of the modern breed, since he was the sire of a number of winning dogs.

By whatever means the results were achieved, the breeders of that period seem to have been skilful at producing smaller and smaller dogs who grew longer and longer coats, but the original objective of a small sporting terrier seems to have been lost sight of. Photographs of 'Ch. Sprig of Blossom' born in 1908 show an animal with a far greater profusion of coat than is usual today and quite unpractical for daily life, let alone catching rats.

The Yorkshire Terrier was sometimes rather scathingly called 'the Dresser Drawer dog' since many fanciers replaced the doors of their cupboards and the front of their dressers with wire netting to form kennels in which their little canine creations lived— their hair carefully parted, oiled and then rolled into innumerable curling papers, their hind feet encased in little socks to avoid damage should they unfortunately desire to scratch. Carefully supervised exercise on the floor or in the garden for the shortest of periods was all that was permitted. However, these little canine prisoners were kept scrupulously clean. The best of food and the benefit of plenty of human company helped to keep their intelligence on the alert.

The life of a show Yorkshire Terrier is not very different at the present time and it is somewhat surprising that they have retained so much of their original sporting character despite the limitations imposed by their curl papers.

A Yorkshire Terrier who leads the life of a normal family dog is extremely active and gay and devoted to his owner to the exclusion of outsiders. The popularity of the breed both in the show ring and as house dogs is increasing steadily.

DESCRIPTION OF THE YORKSHIRE TERRIER

The coat of a Yorkshire Terrier hangs quite straight and evenly down each side, having a parting in the middle, from the nose to the end of the tail. The hair should be as glossy as silk. Much importance is attached to the colour, which should be a dark steel blue, not silver blue, extending from the back of the skull to the root of the tail. The long fall on the head is of a rich golden tan. The chest is a rich bright tan, and the legs are of the same shade. Puppies are born black and tan, the characteristic markings not beginning to show for several months, and a dog may be from a year to a year and a half old by the time he has reached his full beauty. The body is very compact and level on the top of the back. Legs quite straight and well covered with hair; feet as round as possible; tail docked to a medium length. Head rather small and flat, the skull being neither too prominent nor round, and the muzzle not too long. The weight should be under 7 lb.

TERRIERS

Airedale Terriers   *Australian Terriers*

Bedlington Terriers   *Border Terriers*

Bull Terriers   *Cairn Terriers*

Dandie Dinmont Terriers   *Fox Terriers*

Irish Terriers   *Kerry Blue Terriers*

Lakeland Terriers   *Manchester Terriers*

Norwich Terriers   *Scottish Terriers*

Sealyham Terriers   *Skye Terriers*

Staffordshire Bull Terriers   *Welsh Terriers*

West Highland White Terriers

TERRIERS

THE terriers or, as the early writers called them, terroures have never been surrounded by the pomp and circumstance awarded to the hounds: no richly em-
broidered lyammes or leashes, no collars studded with jewels, and lucky if they
got the dregs of the hound's food to eat or a corner of the kennel to sleep in. Terriers are
rarely mentioned in the ancient books on venery and hunting yet they were undoubtedly
around, going to ground after foxes, badgers, otters and polecats and killing the rats and
vermin around the mews and the kennels. Joseph Strutt claimed that the illustrations
to his *Sports and Pastimes of the English People* (1801) were 'engravings selected from
ancient paintings' and 'all copies are faithfully made without the least unnecessary
deviation'. If this be so the fourteenth-century picture of two men at work with spades,
while a presumable fox emerges from a hole and a lean, long-tailed and large-footed
dog leaps after it, can be presumed to be the earliest known representation of a terrier.
Dr Caius (1576) describes the 'terrars' saying 'they . . . creep into the grounde, and by
that means make afrayde, nyppe and bite the Foxe and the Badger in such sorte that
eyther they teare them in pieces with theyr teeth beying in the besome of the earth or
else hayle and pull them perforce out of their lurking angles, dark dungeons, and close
caves . . .'. Nicholas Cox in *The Gentleman's Recreation* (1667) gives a little contemporary information about the appearance of these dogs saying that there are two sorts—
one with crooked legs and short coats and others with longer legs and shaggy coats.
Subsequent writers have repeated these statements without adding much to our knowledge until the Rev. J. Daniel in his *Rural Sports* says '. . . terriers of which there are
two kinds, the one is rough, short-legged, long-backed very strong and most commonly
of a black or yellowish colour mixed with white; the other is smooth-haired and beauti-
fully-formed, having a shorter body and more sprightly appearance, is generally of a
reddish brown colour or black with tanned legs; both these sorts are the determined foe
of all the vermin kind, and in their encounter with the badger very frequently meet with
severe treatment, which they sustain with great courage . . .'.

That is the broad background of the terrier tribe—sporting dogs, living hard in
rural districts, the only criterion for any selective breeding being their tenacity and
working ability, while their work varied according to the type of sport available in the
area in which they lived. It is easy to see how, with little transport and no real reason for
travel, specialised types developed in various parts of the country and it was not until
the changing social conditions of the nineteenth century that the various makes and
shapes of dog were transformed into breeds—most of them signifying by their title the
area or district in which they originated.

109

Airedale Terriers

THE Airedale makes no claim to any particularly ancient line of descent, but he does claim to be the King of Terriers. Originally the Airedales were known as the Waterside Terriers and it was as water dogs that they first found favour with the gamekeepers and sporting fraternity in the neighbourhood of Bradford. Undoubtedly there was terrier blood in their make up, but there is little doubt that it was the Otterhound that gave these dogs their size and strength and liking for water, as well as the big floppy ears that took so much time to breed out.

The earliest breeders of these dogs, many of whom lived in the valley of the Aire, had no thought of the show ring and no particular interest in a dog that would go to ground. What they required was a big, strong dog who would work along the river banks, in and out of the water, tackling anything that might come his way from rats to a dog otter. The fact that a dog of this size and type made an excellent watch and guard dog was just another fact in his favour.

As Waterside or Bingley Terriers these dogs made their first appearance in the show ring in 1883 and three years later they were given their place in the Kennel Club Stud Book with the official title of Airedale Terriers. It took a good few years to produce anything like uniformity of type and to get rid of the large ears and feet that characterised the earlier dogs; to eliminate the soft and open coats that were apt to crop up from time to time as a reminder of the Otterhounds and other anonymous breeds that had had their uses but, by now, were better forgotten.

The fame of these Airedale Terriers spread rapidly, not only all over Great Britain but to America and, as the demand increased, so did the price of winning dogs. A few years earlier two or three pounds would have bought any dog, but by the end of the century the winning 'Master Briar' changed hands for £170.

The first fourteen years of the present century brought the Airedale to his best. Type steadily improved, but the dogs remained real terriers without the exaggerations and artificialities that now tend to spoil so many terrier breeds. Mr Holland Buckley and Mr Mills combined to turn out a succession of winning dogs from their 'Clonmel' kennel and good stock was in demand not only from America, but from Germany, France and Africa and a number of other countries overseas.

After the First World War Airedales continued to be popular favourites for several years, but from 1925 onwards their popularity began to decline. Perhaps the two Airedales who have been most in the public eye during the past twenty-five years are 'Ch. Shelterock Merry Sovereign'—born in the United States, but supreme winner at the Kennel Club Show in 1937—and 'Ch. Riverina Tweedsbairn', the supreme winner at Cruft's in 1961.

110

DESCRIPTION OF THE AIREDALE TERRIER

The back should be short, strong and straight, and the ribs well sprung. Legs perfectly straight with plenty of bone, and feet small and round; eyes small and dark, and neck moderately long and thick without any throatiness. Long head, flat skull, but not too broad between the ears. Ears small and V-shaped. No fulness of cheek and scarcely any stop below the eyes. The jaw deep and powerful, well filled up before the eyes. The tail is set on high and carried gaily without being curled. The coat should be hard and wiry and not long enough to appear ragged; it should be straight and close. The body colour may be black or dark grizzle, with tan on legs, head and ears. The ideal height is between 23 and 24 in. for dogs, bitches slightly less.

111

Australian Terriers

U NTIL comparatively recently Australians have not been interested in dogs except for utilitarian purposes. Small terriers can, however, always make themselves useful and some time late in the last century a liaison between two immigrant terriers may have produced some useful vermin-killing little tykes who found favour around the stables and stockyards and became, in time, the ancestors of the Australian Terriers. It is usually understood that Yorkshire Terriers and the Dandie Dinmont Terriers were the parent stock, but since no records were kept no one knows for certain. With so vast a country and such a mysterious background as well as owners who were not particularly interested in producing dogs with any special uniformity of appearance or definite strain, it is not to be wondered at that the earliest Australian terriers to be seen outside the Continent of their birth varied tremendously in size, shape and colour.

The first overseas journeys made by these little tykes were probably to India for they seemed to have an affinity with the stables and often travelled with the horses that journeyed from Australia to India. Since the dogs were hardy the Indian climate caused them no hardship and they became increasingly popular.

Australian Terriers first appeared in English dog shows in 1906 and in the following year several appeared at a members' show organised by the Ladies' Kennel Association. This event caused some excitement in Australia and the results had to be specially cabled back to the land of their origin. Nevertheless, the breed did not gain a real foothold in this country until about 1921 when Mrs Tebbs imported several dogs from India and Lady Stradbrooke, whose husband had been Governor of Victoria, started a kennel that was to become extremely well known. The Duke of Gloucester had become interested in the breed during the time he was in Australia and has been a patron of the breed ever since.

By 1936 the Australian Terrier was well enough established in this country to be granted championship status and Miss J. Rodochanachi's dog 'Sam of Toorak' became the first English champion.

Undoubtedly the earliest Australian Terriers were uncertain breeding propositions for not only were they apt to throw back to their ancestors but they were often crossed with a collateral relation, the Sydney Silky; and, therefore, it was not easy to eliminate soft coats and produce the desired straight, harsh jacket that the standard requires.

The Australian Terrier has never been among the most popular of the terrier varieties but they have an alert and intelligent outlook on life that should appeal to those who require *multum in parvo*.

DESCRIPTION OF THE AUSTRALIAN TERRIER

The standard describes the dog as being rather low set, compact, active with good straight hair, the harder the better. Coat approximately from 2 to 2½ in. long. Average weight about 10 or 11 lb. Average height about 10 in. The head is long and the skull flat, full between the eyes, with a top-knot of soft hair. Long, powerful jaw with level teeth. Eyes small, keen and dark. Ears small, set high on skull, pricked and free from long hairs. The ears must not be cropped. Neck inclined to be long in proportion to body, with a decided frill of hair. Body rather long in proportion to height; well ribbed up, back straight. Tail docked. Forelegs perfectly straight, set well under body. Slight feather to knee; clean feet. Strong thigh, hocks slightly bent. Feet small and well padded. Colour of body blue or silver-grey, with tan on legs, and blue or silver top-knot. Alternatively, clear sandy or red with soft top-knot.

113

Bedlington Terriers

IT is seldom safe to claim that any breed of dog has an absolutely pure line of descent, since the human race is so often anxious to improve on what they already have by making some addition to it. A cross of this breed or that is made to original stock in order to improve one characteristic or another—sometimes it works and sometimes it does not. The Bedlington Terrier is no exception, but it is possible to trace the original root stock back as far as 1792 with some degree of accuracy, and these are early days for any pedigree to have been recorded, let alone one for a terrier.

These terriers did not take the name of 'Bedlington' until a much later date—probably about 1825—but there is no question that the Northumberland miners and nailers had preserved a type of slim, long-legged, loose-coated and liver-coloured terrier that carried a tuft of hair on its forehead since the eighteenth century, and had always found them invaluable companions on sporting and poaching forays. Such dogs would catch rabbits, rats, marten and, since they were good water dogs, work an otter. What their masters proudly called being 'game' might today be called aggressive, for these dogs were jealous of others and could seldom be worked in pairs, either of their own kind or another. Nevertheless, there were few of the old mining fraternity who would be seen abroad without a terrier of this type at their heels.

The belief that there may have been crosses with the terriers who were later to become known as Dandie Dinmonts is not unlikely since the areas in which the two types flourished were not far apart. The result may have been the crooked forelegs that cursed the longer-legged Northumberland breed for a number of years, while there are one or two names in the earliest of the recorded pedigrees that arouse suspicion.

One of the most famous dogs and the outstanding sire of the nineteenth century was 'Old Piper' or, as he was sometimes known, 'Ainsley's Piper'. Entered to badger when he was a mere eight months old, there was nothing that he would not cope with—otter, badger, foulmart or fox. During his fifteen years of life the old dog dealt with a ferocious sow when it was preparing to attack his master's sleeping child and, shortly before his death when he was almost blind and toothless, he drew a badger that had defeated all the other terriers.

These early Bedlingtons were nearly all liver-coloured with flesh-coloured noses. When these dogs first appeared at shows about 1871 Mr Henry Lacey's 'Miner' was the most frequent winner, but before long it was the blue bitch 'Tyne' and the dog 'Tyneside' that were the show favourites. The Bedlington Terrier Club was formed in 1875. The breed might have reached greater heights of popularity were it not for the difficulty of keeping the linty coat in order—a problem that remains today.

There is no doubt that the Bedlington has brains and is extremely faithful, but he is a difficult dog to keep in show trim and looks shaggy and neglected when left ungroomed. Nevertheless, and regardless of the colour or state of his coat, he remains an excellent sporting terrier.

114

DESCRIPTION OF THE BEDLINGTON TERRIER

Bedlingtons differ in make and shape from other terriers, being more racily built, with a distinctive head formation and carrying their tails intact. The jaws are long, tapering and sharp, and the narrow head is almost in a straight line from the occiput to the nose. These features give what is called a snaky appearance. The body is moderately long and the ribs flat and deep; the back slightly arched, and the tail, which is thick at the root and tapers to a point, is scimitar shaped. The ears, which are filbert shaped, are moderately large and placed flat to the cheek. The silky top-knot to the skull reminds one of the Dandie. The rest of the coat should be hard and twisty with a soft undercoat. The recognised colours are blue, blue-and-tan, liver, and sandy. Height about 16 in.; weight between 18 and 23 lb. The small eyes are well sunk in the head; those of blues should be dark; of blue-and-tan, dark with an amber shade; and the other colours will have light brown eyes.

Border Terriers

THE Border Terrier is not, as some seem to believe, a Scot. He hails from south of the Border, chiefly from Cumberland and Northumberland, and has a long and honourable association with the Border Foxhounds. Furthermore, the Border Terrier is an old breed and it is most unlikely that they are connected with that other Northumberland breed the Bedlington Terrier.

The Robson family has long been associated with Northumberland, the Border Foxhounds and Border Terriers—Mr Jacob Robson swore that there was no better terrier ever born when it came to bolting foxes in rough and rocky country or working in the local wet drains and mossholes. There was certainly no future for any of these terriers unless he was dead game and a willing worker.

There are references to these terriers as far back as 1820. A mustard-coloured dog called 'Flint' is the first of his kind that we hear referred to by name and he is said to have frequently stayed in a hole with a fox for three days at a time and been taken out none the worse. 'Flint' sired 'Rock' and a number of other celebrated workers of the time.

It was 1921 before Border Terriers became a recognised breed with its own Kennel Club register and Challenge Certificates. This was a difficult period in the breed's history for naturally its supporters were anxious that it should not become just another breed of terrier and that its characteristic otter-like head, with its moderately broad skull and strong but short muzzle, should be retained. Judges accustomed to other terrier breeds were apt to look for the more usual long and narrow skull and elongated jaws; it took time and patience to teach them what was required of the breed. Size also formed a bone of contention. It was not many years, however, before the Border Terrier had built a firm place for himself in the affections of those Southeners who admire a sporting terrier.

The outstanding dog of those early show days was Mr Lawrence's 'Ch. Teri', who was not only a notable winner but an excellent sire.

To state that the modern Border Terrier is the replica of those early Northumbrian dogs would not be strictly true, but the physical change is very slight. Anyone who looks at Arthur Wardle's drawing of a group of terriers owned by Mr Robson about 1903 can see that the breed has changed very little in the last sixty years. He certainly retains that bright, alert and lets-get-going expression that has always been a characteristic of these bold little dogs.

A great point in the Border Terrier's favour is his naturalness. His harsh coat needs no trimming and his jaw carries no excessive whisker. Furthermore, the Border is no fighter—in fact he is all that a terrier should be—loyal, intelligent, courageous and hardy.

DESCRIPTION OF THE BORDER TERRIER

The head is not that of the usual show terrier, being otter-shaped—that is moderately broad in skull with short, strong muzzle. Body deep, narrow and fairly long; ribs carried well back but not oversprung, as a terrier should be capable of being spanned by both hands behind the shoulder. Shoulders long and sloping. Forelegs straight, muscular. Feet small and catlike. The short undocked tail is carried gaily. Coat hard, with a good undercoat. Colours red, wheaten, grizzle, tan or blue-and-tan. Eyes dark. Small drop ears, V-shaped. Approved weights are from 13 to $15\frac{1}{2}$ lb. for dogs, $11\frac{1}{2}$ to 14 lb. for bitches.

Bull Terriers

THE early Bull Terriers, depicted by a number of early seventeenth-century sporting artists, was exactly what the name implies—a cross between a bull dog and some form of terrier. Their virtue lay more in their courage than in their appearance. Organised dog fighting was a popular but bestial sport—merely to read the rules is enough to make anyone of the present day feel sick.

Those fighting dogs were demons in their way, but one has to admire them for their courage and tenacity. Usually fawn, brindle or smut in colour; crop-eared and whip-tailed, the most powerful of them were employed to kill their own kind or themselves be killed, while the lighter or smaller types found employment in the rat pits where the onlookers would wager large sums of money on the number of rats the dog could kill in a given time. A good dog for his purpose was highly valued and Lord Camelford paid £84 for the dog he presented to Jem Belcher in order 'that the best fighting biped should own the champion fighting quadruped'. The brindled dog 'Pincher' who weighed a mere 25 lb. and was owned by Billy Shaw killed 500 rats in 36 minutes 26½ seconds in March, 1865.

It is to James Hinks, a dog dealer of Birmingham, that we are mainly indebted for the production of the modern white Bull Terrier. James Hinks started on his task about 1850 and it is fairly clear that he crossed the old heavy type of Bull Terrier with the terriers once known as the White English Terriers. The first results of Hinks' breeding activities were 'Madman' and 'Puss', both of them prize winners of their time. Some 'doggy' men taunted Hinks saying that the white and more refined terriers were soft and could not fight. 'Can't they?' replied Hinks and there and then matched 'Puss', who had that very day won a first prize at a show, against a short-faced dog of the same weight for a stake of £5 and a case of champagne. The fight took place that night at the famous Tuppers in Long Acre. The next morning 'Puss' was back on her bench at the show, her opponent dead, and Mr Hinks richer by £5.

The early stud book entries are both confusing and inaccurate with 'Madmen', 'Victors' and 'Rebels' appearing not once but many times and in a variety of ownerships. The early history of the breed is far from being a fair page of an open book, but the breed had a steadily increasing public for it became the 'done' thing for undergraduates and subalterns to be seen about with a white or nearly white Bull Terrier. The abolition of ear cropping in 1895 caused difficulties for the breed and many of the old fanciers declared that it was ruined, but it was not long before careful breeding produced a naturally erect ear and the Bull Terrier remained a popular companion.

The present day standard of Bull Terrier points makes use of the expression 'gladiator' when describing these dogs—thereby suggesting arenas and fights to the death. The Bull Terrier is certainly a virile and powerful dog who requires discipline and careful training, but he is also a sensible and often amusingly clownish dog who makes an admirable guard and companion. As in the old days there are large and small Bull Terriers and the miniatures should weigh under 18 lb. They should certainly be better known than they are.

DESCRIPTION OF THE BULL TERRIER

The head is one of the most conspicuous features of the breed. In profile it should be down-faced, almost forming an arc from the occiput to the nose, and the line is not broken by stop or indentation. The foreface must be filled right up to the eyes. The forehead is fairly flat and not domed between the ears. The foreface is longer than the forehead, and the muzzle should show great strength. The ears are small and thin, placed on the top of the skull fairly close together, and are either erect or erectile. The body shows enormous power and activity. It should be short, with great muscular development, the shoulders strong and muscular, with no dip at the withers. Chest broad and deep and ribs well sprung. Legs should have plenty of bone without being coarse and should be perfectly straight. The tail, thick at the root and tapering to a fine point, is carried horizontally. The present-day Miniature is a sound, well-balanced Terrier about $12\frac{1}{2}$ in. in height with plenty of substance and bone, weighing under 18 lb. Otherwise identical in appearance with its cousin.

Cairn Terriers

ALL the terriers of Scotland have much in common in both character and structure —their admirers call them 'determined' and their detractors call them plain 'obstinate'. They are all plucky and active with the strong, short legs that enable them to dig and go to ground in seemingly impossible places, while their coats are harsh and weather resistant.

The terriers now called Cairns developed mainly in the Hebrides and Western Highlands; they had worked there for many generations before a few individuals made their way south in the early years of the twentieth century. At the end of the last century and in the early years of the present Captain Allan Macdonald of Waternish, on the western coast of Skye, owned a pack of game, short-legged terriers with which he hunted fox and otter in all parts of Skye, Uist and North and South Harris.

Mrs Alastair Campbell was one of the first people to introduce these little northern terriers to a wider sphere. Since the newcomers were then called 'short-haired Skye Terriers' the supporters of the Skye breed rose in their wrath and unwittingly provided the little strangers with considerable and useful publicity. This all took place about 1908; the battle raged for a year or more and peace was restored only in 1909 when the official title of the breed became Cairn Terrier. The years that followed were eventful and saw a great deal of progress—Kennel Club registrations showed a steady increase year by year and in 1911 the Cairn Terrier Club was formed. Lady Sophie Scott's bitch 'Tibbie of Harris' became the breed's first champion and she was soon joined by Mrs Alastair Campbell's dog 'Ch. Gesto'. In 1914 the late Baroness Burton's 'Dochfour' kennel began to show the first signs of developing the influence that was to become so great and so beneficial in future years.

From the end of 1914 until 1918 breeding restrictions prevented any further progress, but once the First World War was over there was a tremendous wave of interest in dogs and the Cairn breed were not slow to benefit from it. Such hardy and charming little dogs could not be overlooked by other dog-loving countries and it was not long before there was a considerable demand from the United States and many other countries in both hemispheres for good specimens.

The Cairn Terriers of today do not vary much from the Cairn Terriers of the past and anyone shown a photograph of a dog taken around 1908 would have little or no difficulty in recognising its breed. In character and constitution these little dogs remain hardy, intelligent, affectionate and sporting and wear coats that need the minimum of trimming to keep them neat and tidy. There is no reason to wonder why the Cairns are now the most popular of all the terrier breeds.

120

DESCRIPTION OF THE CAIRN TERRIER

The Cairn's head is smallish, skull broad in proportion and fox-like in general shape. The erect ears are small and pointed and not set very closely together. The tail is carried gaily, but should not curl over the back. Legs of medium length and not too heavy in bone. The coat is hard but not coarse, and there is a thick undercoat. The body is compact and straight, with well-sprung ribs. The colours are various, from brindle, grey-brindle, grey, red or nearly black. Dark points such as ears and muzzle are typical of the breed.

Dandie Dinmont Terriers

T HE Dandie Dinmont has the distinction of being the only breed of dog named after a character in fiction. Very few people had ever heard or thought of these dogs until Sir Walter Scott published *Guy Mannering* in 1814 with its description of Dandie Dinmont, the Border farmer, who owned and worked a pack of hard bitten, short legged, round skulled terriers whose rough coats were described as being either mustard or pepper in colour. The Dandie Dinmont described by Sir Walter called all his dogs 'Auld Pepper' or 'Auld Mustard', 'Young Pepper' or 'Young Mustard' and 'Little Pepper' and 'Little Mustard'. It was commonly believed that Sir Walter had a well-known Border sporting character—James Davidson of Hyndlee—in mind when he described Dandie Dinmont and his dogs. This, however, he denied, saying that the character was entirely imaginary. This may have been so, but the dogs definitely were not. Sir Walter had probably seen numbers of them in the days of his boyhood spent at Sandyknowe.

Guy Mannering was widely read and it was not surprising that it aroused a great deal of interest in the terriers who were so well described but, naturally, were of a rougher and tougher type than those we know today.

The Duke of Buccleuch, the Hon. G. H. Baillie of Mellerstain, John Stoddard of Selkirk and J. B. Richardson of Dumfries as well as Mr Bradshaw Smith of Ecclefechan, all played a part in establishing the terrier breed that was at first facetiously known as Dandie Dinmont Terriers and, later, adopted the title in all seriousness.

The Dandie Dinmonts did not have a very peaceful passage—in fact, they had a very stormy ten years getting themselves established and accepted in the world outside the Border country. In 1867 Mr M. Smith refused to award prizes to the dogs on show at Birmingham saying that the whole lot were mongrels. These were hard words and although they broke no bones they started a long, verbose, but to us today interesting, argument from which an exceedingly vivid picture of the Border life at the beginning of the century emerges.

Around 1872 'Peachem' was one of the outstanding dogs of his race. He belonged to the brothers Robert and Paul Scott of Jedburgh who were itinerant pedlars. When Robert brought 'Peachem' to the south of England and showed him at the Crystal Palace he not only won praise and awards but he aroused considerable interest and it was felt that this dog approached the type that had found favour at the beginning of the century.

Undoubtedly the modern Dandie Dinmonts are more *svelte* and tailored than those of the old days, but character does not appear to have suffered a great deal. The Dandie remains gentle and affectionate in his home but determined to defend it against all strangers whether they have two legs or four. Given the opportunity he is game and sporting—unfortunately he is only too seldom presented with the necessary 'opportunity'. There is no terrier breed that produces puppies of greater charm—their large, round speculative eyes shine from under little fluffy pates, soon to be crowned with the breed's typical top knot, and one forgets the damaged slippers, the tunnels under the lawn and the strange hairlessness of the cat's tail as they roll on their backs and suggest that their tummies would be the better for a nice scratch.

DESCRIPTION OF THE DANDIE DINMONT TERRIER

The Dandie Dinmont's head looks big for his size, though it should not be out of proportion. The profuse, soft, silky hair on the crown accentuates this peculiarity. The jaws are powerful, equipped with formidable teeth that will kill rats with celerity. The rich, dark, hazel eyes betoken intelligence and dignity. The ears are set low and hang close to the cheeks. The neck is muscular and well developed. The body is long and flexible, with well-sprung ribs and round chest, the latter being well let down between the forelegs. The back, rather low at the shoulders, arches over the loins and then makes a gradual drop. The tail is curved like a scimitar. The front legs are short and very strong, being well equipped with bone and muscle. The hind legs are a trifle longer and are placed rather wide apart. The coat, from the skull to the root of the tail, is a mixture of hardish and soft hair, which gives it a pily feeling. That on the under part of the body is light in colour and softer. Colours may be either pepper or mustard; the former ranging from a dark bluish black to a light silver grey. Mustards vary from a reddish brown to a pale fawn.

Fox Terriers

FOX Terriers were largely the dogs of the stable and the kennels: no great concern of anyone except to be whistled up when there was a rat around or to go ferreting with the stable lads or join in the excitement when the ricks were being threshed. Puppies were generally reared behind a bale of straw and changed hands for a shilling or two as soon as they were weaned. In the hunting stables the kennel terriers were a little better off. A good terrier or two ran with most packs of hounds and if the fox went to ground they were expected to be on hand to bolt it.

One hears little of white terriers until the appearance of *The Sportsman's Cabinet* in 1803 where the illustrator, Philip Reinagle, gives an excellent picture of terriers at work—one of whom is white with a patched head and a mark at the root of the tail. The author of the book, T. Taplin, tells us something of this white terrier who, he says, is the dam of wonderful progeny, 'seven of whom sold recently for one and twenty guineas'.

There was not much to be seen of Fox Terriers at the earliest dog shows. A pedigree-less dog called 'Trimmer' headed a class of twenty at a show held at Islington in 1862, but later that year at Birmingham there was a class for 'White and other smooth-haired English Terriers, except Black-and-Tan'. Here there were twenty-four entries and the winner was 'Jock', exhibited by Mr Thomas Wootton of Nottingham.

'Jock', known to all students of Fox Terrier pedigrees as 'Old Jock', together with 'Old Trap'—the dog who had stood second to him that day at Birmingham—and 'Old Tartar' were the great dogs of their time. They were the ancestors of most of the great Fox Terriers who were to follow.

'Old Jock' had been born in either the Grove or the Quorn kennel. Mr Wootton bought the dog for £5 and sold him on at least two occasions for sums approaching £100. 'Jock' was a good ratter, would tackle a vixen single handed, and had won a great number of prizes. He sired many good terriers and was so highly esteemed that the Rev. Jack Russell, that strict terrier man and excellent judge, twice mated him to his wire-coated bitches. 'Trap' and 'Tartar' both had somewhat doubtful pedigrees, but both of them were game and sporting terriers. 'Grove Nettle' is perhaps the most famous of the early bitches and best deserves the claim to the title of Mother of the breed.

It was 1873 before the wire-haired variety of Fox Terrier got their own classes at shows and at first these were classified as a 'non-sporting' breed. This, not unnaturally, caused a considerable outcry and the matter was rectified. 'Venture' and 'Tip' were the two outstanding dogs of this period.

The popularity of both Smooth-coated and Wire-haired Fox Terriers faded somewhat in the first years of the present century, but by the 1920s the Wire-haired variety was at the peak of its career. Not only was there a great demand for dogs as pets and companions, but large prices were paid for dogs to go to the United States, where their popularity was as great as it was here. Since then Fox Terriers of both coats have had up-and-down careers. The true working conditions for a Fox Terrier are now seldom available, but, even if they were, there are few modern terriers who could equal the career and performance of 'Old Jock' even if they were allowed to try.

DESCRIPTION OF THE FOX TERRIER

The Smooth Fox Terrier has bone and strength in small compass, without clumsiness or coarseness. Legs must be of the right length—neither too long nor too short. Though his back is short, straight and strong, he stands over a lot of ground, and he should be up on his toes all the time, full of fire and dash, with stern carried gaily. He should be big enough to run with hounds, and small enough to go to ground. Weight should be approximately 15 to 17 lb. for a bitch and 16 to 18 lb. for a dog, in show condition. The skull is flat, instead of rounded, moderately narrow, and gradually decreasing in width to the eyes. The jaws are strong and muscular, instead of short and pointed. The small, dark eyes are rather deep set. The front legs are dead straight, showing scarcely any ankle, and strong in bone. Feet small, round and compact; coat smooth, hard, dense and abundant. The Wire-Haired Fox Terrier's coat should neither look nor feel woolly and there should be no silky hair about the skull or elsewhere, nor should the coat be long enough to give a shaggy appearance. The best coats are of a dense, dry texture—like coconut matting—the hairs growing closely and strongly together; when parted with the fingers the skin cannot be seen. At the base of the stiff hairs is a shorter growth of finer and softer hair—the undercoat. The coat on the sides is never quite so hard as that on the back and quarters. The colour of the coat is of little importance, but white should predominate; brindle; liver or slate blue is objectionable. A fully-grown dog should not measure more than $15\frac{1}{2}$ in. to the withers and should weigh about 18 lb.; bitches should be proportionately smaller.

125

Irish Terriers

IRELAND has produced numerous breeds of dog, several of them of the terrier fraternity: perhaps the best-known is the Irish Terrier. These dogs were first heard of in this country when they appeared at Glasgow show in 1875 and again at Brighton a year later, but they were undoubtedly a very old Irish breed. These were not quite the terriers we know today for their necks were thick and coarse, their ears were cropped and their tails docked short; in fact they lacked the elegance we expect of our present-day dogs with their small and velvety ears, tails that are long enough to balance their bodies and slim graceful necks that support the narrow skulled and long muzzled head.

The years from 1875 onwards were a time of rapid advancement and the Irish Terrier Club was formed in 1879 and laid down a standard of points that is basically the same as the one in use today. In 1889 the Irish Terrier Club requested the Kennel Club to ban ear cropping and this request was acceded to, and it was not long before the practice was abolished altogether.

Two notable Irish Terriers were firstly Killiney Boy, bred by Mr Burke of Dublin, from whom he passed to a Mr Flanaghan who appears to have lost or abandoned the dog, for he was found by Mr Donnegan who gave him to Mr Howard Waterhouse in whose ownership he appeared at Belfast Show and caused a minor sensation. The second was the bitch 'Erin', owned by Mr W. Graham, who made her first appearance at the Alexandra Palace Show in 1879 and rapidly became a champion. 'Erin' was the finest Irish Terrier to have been seen up to that time, but an even more remarkable brood bitch. She was mated to 'Killiney Boy' on two or three occasions and in their first litter they produced 'Poppy', 'Playboy', 'Pretty Lass', 'Pagan II', 'Gerald' and 'Peggy', all of whom were to have an influence on the future of the breed. The first four became champions and 'Playboy' and 'Poppy' were constant rivals. A repeat of the mating produced 'Droleen', who when mated to a son of 'Pagan II' became the dam of the famous 'Ch. Brickbat', who won the Challenge Cup offered by the Irish Terrier Club twelve times in succession.

The Irish Terrier breed was extremely popular up to the time of the First World War, but unlike most of the other breeds it did not recover after the Armistice. By 1930 the breed was in a very poor position and even an exhibition of many of the best dogs of the day, staged at Selfridges and given a great deal of publicity, did little or nothing to drag the breed from the doldrums. The trouble can be traced to the exaggerated belief that these Irish dogs were terrible fighters. In these overcrowded days a fighting dog is no pleasure to own, but generally speaking the Irishman is no worse than many other terriers, and even when he does 'trail the tail of his coat' one should forgive him because of his faithfulness and enormous amount of Irish charm. At the present time the Irish Terrier has a steady and reliable circle of admirers, but like most of the terrier breeds his popularity is only numerically moderate.

DESCRIPTION OF THE IRISH TERRIER

The most desirable weight is about 27 lb. for a dog and 25 lb. for a bitch. They are somewhat higher on the leg than Fox Terriers, and also more racily built. They are expected to present 'an active, lively, lithe, and wiry appearance; lots of substance, at the same time free of clumsiness, as speed and endurance, as well as power, are very essential.' Front legs should have plenty of bone and muscle, and should be quite straight. Shoulders long and sloping, and chest deep and muscular without being full or wide. The back is moderately long, and it should be strong and straight. Loins broad and powerful, and slightly arched; ribs deep rather than round. The neck is a fair length, and the head is long, with a skull that is flat, and rather narrow between the ears, which are small and V-shaped. Eyes a dark hazel colour, small and not prominent. Whole coloured bright red, red-wheaten, or yellow-red, are the preferable colours, and the coat should be hard and wiry.

127

Kerry Blue Terriers

T HE Kerry Blue Terrier of today is a very different dog from the first Kerry Blue Terriers to appear at English shows about 1920. Where the Kerry Blue had been before this time is something of a mystery, since County Kerry itself was not very anxious to acknowledge the breed. Nevertheless, Mr Charles Galway of Waterford is said to have long owned a strain of game blue or black terriers whose coat was inclined to curl and with which he would never part. It has been said that the extinct 'gadhar' or Irish herding dog may have been an ancestor of these terriers and there has been a faint suggestion that these soft-coated terriers of Ireland were occasionally used for working sheep as well as for fighting and ratting.

It was somewhere about 1911 that the first effort to 'tidy up' the blue terriers was made and it was probably then that an infusion of Bedlington Terrier blood was introduced, most probably with the intention of improving the texture of the Kerry's coat and its colour. If it had not been for the First World War these Kerry Blue Terriers would probably have been seen at English shows earlier than they were. It was at Cruft's in 1922 that the breed made its first public appearance and somewhat later when it became eligible for Challenge Certificates. The first dogs to win Certificates were Mrs E. A. Green's Irish-bred 'Martell's Sapphire Beauty', and Mrs Casey Hewitt's bitch 'Belle of Munster'. In 1924 and Earl of Kenmare exhibited a bitch he had bought from an Irish farmer, whose name of 'Kenmare Molly' soon became 'Ch. Kenmare Molly' since she won the Challenge Certificate at nine of the ten shows where she was exhibited. One of the greatest dogs ever to appear on the benches was Mrs Handy's 'Ch. Princetown Hell-of-a-Fellow' who won every breed honour in the years that preceded 1939.

There was never any excuse for ennui at any of the early shows where the Kerry Blues were exhibited—one heard the battles long before one saw the dogs and there was no such thing as a private fight between two exhibits; the first wry word was a sign for it to become a public affair at which all were welcome. Those days are over and the Kerry Blue is now no more aggressive than any other terrier. But during the process of taming he has lost a lot of his charm, for the lovely dark or silvery blue natural coat and the overhanging eyebrows that once shaded such twinkling, humorous Irish eyes are seen no more.

To put a modern Kerry Blue in the ring needs hours and hours of work with clippers, scissors and trimming knife; except for the Poodle there is no breed that receives more attention from the canine coiffeuse. Barbering has not spoilt the dog's nature—sinners they may be, but they have a strong sense of humour and are loyal, faithful and affectionate and, if given the chance, make good guards and excellent workmen.

DESCRIPTION OF THE KERRY BLUE TERRIER

The head is long and flat over the skull; the jaw very strong and deep; eyes dark brown or dark hazel. The body is of moderate length, with straight, strong back; loins broad and powerful and deep; hindquarters strong and muscular, with powerful thighs; front legs straight, with plenty of bone. Weight is from 33 to 37 lb. Up to the present the colour, although nominally blue, has varied a great deal, some nearly black dogs being exhibited. The Dublin Club have decided that more attention should be paid to colour, the endeavour being to get a light silver, dark silver, or inky blue. Up to the age of eighteen months slight tan markings are allowable, but after that age they should disappear.

Lakeland Terriers

HERE again we have a breed of terrier that has developed entirely within the boundaries of a district where it is the custom for the terriers to run with the foxhounds who, in this Fell district, are hunted on foot. It is obvious then that it is a tough but active little dog that is required and both his courage and his powers of endurance must be beyond suspicion. A dog already exhausted by hunting across the rocky hills of his native country would be useless when expected to go underground and bolt a wiry Lakeland fox.

The Lakeland Terriers of today were previously known by various titles—Fell Terriers, Cumberland or Westmorland Terriers being but a trio of them.

Although the Lakeland Terrier has never laid claim to an ancient lineage the fact remains that these little dogs—almost, but not quite, the smallest of the terriers—greatly resemble the terriers to be seen in a number of old prints. The modern dogs are probably somewhat more refined in type, while their skulls are narrower and the legs straighter, but a remarkably strong resemblance between old and new remains.

A working terrier has to be not only game but fit, for it has been estimated that the hounds often travel forty miles or so in a day up the hills and down the dales. If the fox disappears down into a crevice or drain or into an earth beneath a boulder, the terrier has to follow, and if the fox refuses to bolt, then the terrier will have to tackle and kill it although it may be larger than himself. It is because the dogs may have to negotiate such narrow crevices and work in such cramped space that it is essential that they are narrower chested than other terriers and anywhere their heads will go their bodies should be capable of following.

It was not until 1928 that Lakeland Terriers were seen at a show in the south of England. Before that it was rare for them to make public appearances except at local hound shows held in and around their native Lake District. In 1921 the Lakeland Terrier Association had been formed with the idea of improving the type and Lord Lonsdale, whose family had kept these terriers for fifty years or more, became the association's first president.

Mr Paisley, Mr H. L. Tweedie and Mrs Graham Spence were the pioneer breeders and exhibitors of these terriers and it was Mr Tweedie's dog 'Evergreen's Double' and Mrs Spence's bitch 'Lady of the Lake' who subsequently won the first Challenge Certificates offered for the breed. Mrs Spence was one of the strongest supporters of the breed and very wisely maintained that breeders should always remember that the Lakeland was a working terrier before it was a show dog.

130

DESCRIPTION OF THE LAKELAND TERRIER

Lakeland Terriers have to be fairly compact, strong and agile, with frames that enable them to squeeze through narrow apertures, and sufficient length of leg for them to run with hounds or jump on to the ledges on which the fox may take refuge. Colour may be blue, blue-and-tan, black-and-tan, red, liver, wheaten, grizzle or black; small tips of white on feet and chest do not debar. Weight of dogs 17 lb., bitches 15 lb. Height should not exceed 14½ in. The skull should be well balanced, flat and refined, the muzzle should be broad but not too long and the jaws powerful. A black nose is preferred. The ears should be moderately small, V-shaped, and carried alertly. The eyes should be dark or hazel. The chest reasonably narrow, the back strong, moderately short and well coupled. The neck should be large but in proportion to the body, the forelegs straight, the feet round, compact and well padded. The coat should be dense and weather-resisting, harsh and with a good undercoat. The tail well set on, carried gaily, but not to curl over the back.

131

Manchester Terriers

THE Manchester Terrier was originally and more correctly known as the Black-and-Tan Terrier. Undoubtedly this breed of terrier bears some resemblance to terriers of the earliest known type and may well carry a few drops of their blood. The misguided efforts of early Victorian fanciers, especially those of the Manchester area, to 'smarten 'em up' has produced a more lightly built dog with a wonderful uniformity of markings and neat whip tails, but it has spoilt them as working terriers.

The original Black-and-Tan Terriers had strong jaws, heavy skulls and rather thick tails—sometimes docked and sometimes not—and ears that might or might not be cropped but were usually natural. No one much minded whether the coat was rough or smooth or how much of the dog was black and how much tan. From the moment these terriers began to appear at dog shows their deterioration as working terriers began. The fanciers decreed that the coat markings must be exact to the pattern they laid down—on the head the muzzle had to be tanned to the nose but the nose itself and the nasal bone had to be black. There was to be a small black 'kissing' spot on each black cheek and others over the eyes, while a tan 'V' ran from under the jaw and down the throat and two slight tan marks had to appear on the chest. The front legs from below the knee were to be tan, but the toes were to be pencilled with black and a black 'thumb' mark should appear just above the feet. Inside the hind legs there were to be tan markings but divided with black at the stifle joint. The underside of the tail also had to be tan and a narrow strip at the vent.

Broadly speaking this is the pattern on which nature distributed black and tan on a number of breeds and obviously a clear bright tan and a glossy black is preferable to either wishy-washy or rusty colourings. But the over-emphasis on exactitude of their placings ended in all other points being subordinated to this fad and led first to the faking and dyeing of the dogs, then to general dissatisfaction with the breed and ultimately to a steady decline in its popularity. In 1860 an entry of three score or so dogs at a large show was far from uncommon: in 1902 a mere half dozen appeared at the Crystal Palace Show. In justice, it must be admitted that the abolition of ear cropping had been a blow to the breed, but Manchester Terriers mostly had small, well dropped ears and what was sauce for the goose was sauce for the gander since a number of other breeds had the same ban to contend with and did so successfully.

By 1939 the breed was in a very precarious position with Miss Schwabe as its principal supporter and the war years did nothing to help a very critical situation. Somehow the breed was saved from extinction, for from the middle of the present century onwards the situation began to improve slightly and its previously very low fertility rate began to rise. At the present time the breed has a small but enthusiastic band of supporters and although no longer of much use as a working terrier the Manchester makes an extremely pleasant and intelligent family dog with a good chance of becoming more widely appreciated in the years to come.

DESCRIPTION OF THE MANCHESTER TERRIER

Manchester Terriers should be compact in appearance with good bone. The head to be long with flat, narrow skull, wedge-shaped with tapering, tight-lipped jaws. The ears small and V-shaped carried well above the top line of the head. Mouth level. Neck long and tapering from the shoulder to head with an arched crest. Shoulders should be clean and sloping. Forelegs quite straight and of proportionate length to the dog. Short body with well-sprung ribs, slightly arched and well cut up behind the ribs. The feet should be small and strong with well-arched toes. Tail short and set on where arch of back ends, thick where it joins the body, carried not higher than the level of the back. The coat is close, smooth, short and glossy of jet black and mahogany colour distributed in a well established pattern. Weight 17 or 18 lb.

133

Norwich Terriers

THE Norwich Terrier is a real little cocktail of a dog, full of spirits and bounce. He is a very modern production whose assorted ancestors vary a great deal in make and shape. Nevertheless, the Norwich Terrier now breeds quite true to type, although it is up to those that breed them to decide whether they prefer their little dogs to have prick ears or drop ears, since either are permissible, although the two varieties are not usually inter-bred.

The Norwich Terrier should weigh between 11 lb. and 12 lb. and thus he is the smallest of the terriers. There is, however, a tendency at the present time to breed them rather larger which seems a pity since it is as 'much in little' that they really excel.

Even though the Norwich Terrier is such a modern production no one seems quite sure how the breed was built up and accounts vary considerably. Without question Mr Jodrell Hopkins, a horse dealer who lived at Trumpington near Cambridge and, later, at Newmarket, played a big part and his little smooth coated bitch acquired at the time of the South African War seems to have been the Eve from whom the breed sprang. Her little vermin-chasing offspring were always in great demand by sporting under-graduates. Mr Hopkins' employee Mr Frank Jones was also keen on these little terriers and crossed them with this and that dog, always providing they were small and game. Small Irish Terriers and Glen of Imaal Terriers are two breeds frequently mentioned. Mr Stokes of Market Harborough, Mr Nichols of Wymondham and Mr Cooke, the Master of the Norwich Staghounds, all had dogs of the Hopkins strain and it was Mr Stokes who when asked what breed his little terrier belonged to replied 'Trumpington Terrier', thus adding another provisional title to a type of terrier sometimes already referred to as a 'Jones Terrier'. As time went on there was an increasingly ready market both here and overseas for these hard working, game little tykes who would follow a horse all day, go to ground when asked, tackle a fox or a rat and go home at night with their minute tails still in the air.

By 1914 Mrs Fagan was breeding methodically from a bitch directly descended from dogs owned by Mr Jones, and from these 'Jerico Hill' dogs descend a great number of the Norwich Terriers we see around today.

By 1932 these little East Anglian terriers were sufficiently popular and sufficiently numerous for the Kennel Club to allow them to appear at shows and a short three years later they gained full championship status.

One cannot claim that these early show dogs were a level lot—not unnaturally they varied considerably in size and shape. Nevertheless, and despite Mr Jones' gloomy prophecies, the Norwich Terrier has remained a small, sharp, intelligent, loyal and active little terrier with a particular penchant for horses and the stable yard.

Among the many virtues of a breed, whose climb to considerable heights of public favour was rapid, is the fact that the harsh and wiry coat typical of the breed needs no barbering to keep its owner looking smart and tidy.

DESCRIPTION OF THE NORWICH TERRIER

The standard aims at a dog that shall weigh between 11 and 12 lb. Height should not exceed 10 in. at withers. The muzzle is foxy yet strong, the length being about one-third less than a measurement from the occiput to the bottom of the stop, which should be well defined. Skull wide, slightly rounded, and having good width between eyes and between ears. Ears, if erect, slightly larger than a Cairn's; if dropped, very neat and small. Eyes very dark, bright and keen, full of expression.

Teeth strong and rather large. Neck short and strong, set on clean shoulders. Back short to medium; loins very strong; ribs well sprung. Legs short, powerful, straight if possible with sound bone. Feet round and thick. Quarters strong, with great powers of propulsion. Tail docked to a medium length. Colour—red, red-wheaten, black-and-tan or brindle being permitted. Coat as hard and wiry as possible and absolutely straight, lying close to the body.

Scottish Terriers

ALL the native terriers of Scotland are in some degree related. Since their work is similar whether they developed in Skye or Aberdeen, they are all short legged, have a fair length of back, strong jaws and weather-resisting coats: with the possible exception of the Skye Terrier, whose ears may rise or fall, and the Dandie Dinmont, whose ears always drop, all of Scotland's terriers have prick ears. The Scotties' short, strong legs enable them to dig in rough, hard country and their low-to-ground bodies permit them to enter cavities between boulders and rocks of their native hills, while their fair length of back enables them to turn round within a limited space. Prick ears are said to enhance hearing and the uses for strong teeth and jaws and harsh coats are obvious.

Without giving offence a Scottish Terrier may be referred to as a 'Scottie' but never as an 'Aberdeen'. The erroneous, but not unusual, belief of those ignorant of Scottish Terrier history that these dogs are Aberdonians probably arises from the fact that Mr Adamson of Aberdeen owned one of the leading kennels at a period when these dogs were first claiming public attention as show and companion dogs.

The earliest show Scotties who appeared in classes for 'Yorkshire and broken-haired terriers' or 'Scotch and Yorkshire Terriers' were somewhat higher on their rather crooked legs and much shorter in muzzle than they were to become within the next few years. According to Mr Thompson Gray, whose monograph *The Dogs of Scotland*, published in 1887, gives an account of Captain Mackie's search for the best working terriers of a type required for founding a kennel, Argyll and Perthshire produced the best dogs. But quite certainly terriers much resembling the modern Scottie have been known for many centuries.

Scottish Terriers first appeared at a show held south of the Border in 1879. At the Kennel Club's own show in that year the dog 'Tartan' and the bitch 'Splinter II' were the chief prize winners. The mating of these two and a subsequent mating of 'Splinter II' with a dog called 'Bonaccord' produced a male line from which every living Scottish Terrier descends through the half-brothers 'Ch. Dundee' and 'Ch. Alister' who were both grandsons of 'Splinter'. Another stalwart of a slightly later date was 'Ch. Rascal', a grandson of 'Ch. Dundee'.

Slowly and steadily Scottish Terriers became more uniform in shape and size and the years between 1929 and 1937 were probably the hey-day of the breed. A dog originally called 'Snookers Double' came into the hands of Mr R. Chapman who changed his name —as the regulations then allowed—to 'Heather Necessity'. 'Necessity' had the longest and strongest head yet seen on a Scottie as well as the outstanding personality that soon made him 'Ch. Heather Necessity', one of the great dogs of his time and a notable sire with eighteen champion grandchildren.

As a companion the Scottie remains what he always has been—slightly dour with strangers but with a strong, determined character that makes him one of the most loyal and amusing of all the dogs on the canine register.

DESCRIPTION OF THE SCOTTISH TERRIER

The head is long, with punishing jaws. Small eyes of a dark brown or hazel colour. Ears small and erect, pointed at the tips. The neck is short, thick and muscular, but set strongly into the sloping shoulder. Chest comparatively broad and deep in proportion. Body of moderate length and rather flat-sided. Legs short and very heavy in bone, the front ones being straight and set well under the body. In the back legs the hocks should be bent and the thighs very muscular; feet strong and small. The tail is never docked. The coat is rather short, being about 2 in. long, very hard and wiry in texture and dense all over the body. Colours black, wheaten or brindle. The ideal weight is 19 to 23 lb., the height 10 to 11 in.

Sealyham Terriers

WHETHER Captain Edwardes of Sealy Ham in Wales would approve of the terriers that now carry the name of his estate is very doubtful since Captain Edwardes was a hard taskmaster and a man who did not care for pedigrees, let alone dog shows or terriers as house pets. He simply required a short-legged white dog who would tackle anything either above or below ground. The emphasis on a white dog arose from the fact that brown or darker coloured dogs were apt to be mistaken for a fox by the hounds, and on the short legs so that the dogs could work in drains and earths.

The year 1860 is usually said to be the one in which Captain Edwardes began his breeding operations, but what he had against the existing types of Fox Terrier history does not relate. Presumably Jack Russell's sporting strain of Fox Terriers were too high on the leg for a dog that was not intended to run with hounds and was intended mainly for badger digging and, presumably, the small white terriers from the western side of Scotland had not come to Captain Edwardes' notice. The first cross appears to have been between a local type of terrier and the local short-legged cattle dogs—the original Corgi stock. The later introduction of Dandie Dinmont blood confirmed the short-leggedness and added tenacity and a deep hound-like voice. To this was added 'Cheshire Terrier' blood: no one quite knows what a Cheshire Terrier was, but it is generally believed to have been a strain of Bull Terrier. This mixture of Welsh, Scottish and North Country breeds appears to have served the required purpose, but Captain Edwardes had high and harsh standards. His puppies were put out to walk with tenants and keepers. When their owner visited them he was always accompanied by two hard bitten and hard biting terriers and his gun. If the puppies did not stand their ground against the belligerent visitors they were shot out of hand.

Captain Edwardes' terriers gained fame in their own locality and passed into other hands; but it is obvious that it would be some time before dogs of such mixed ancestry would breed true to a definite type. Captain Edwardes died before his terriers became popular favourites, not only in this country and the U.S., but everywhere that a good terrier was appreciated. The originator of the breed would certainly have had no use for the trimming and barbering that the modern Sealyham has to undergo before he appears in the show ring.

It was 1910 when Sealyham Terriers made their first appearance at the Kennel Club Show. Lord Kensington's 'Dandy Bach' and 'St Bride's Delight' won the Open dog and the Open bitch class, while Messrs Lewis and Gwyther's dog 'Peer Gynt', who had only won a reserve award, changed hands for £50 and went on to become one of the most famous sires in the history of the breed.

The craze for Sealyham Terriers that once swept over both England and the United States has faded slightly, but no dog that is so gay, humorous and devoted could be allowed to fade from the scene and those that have once owned a Sealyham generally remain faithful to the breed.

DESCRIPTION OF THE SEALYHAM TERRIER

The skull is wide between the ears, the jaw is powerful, and the body is long. The coat is hard and profuse. Eyes are dark brown or dark hazel. The neck is fairly long, thick and muscular, and the chest is broad and deep, being well let down between the legs. Ribs are well sprung, and the hindquarters are very strong. The body should be sufficiently long to be flexible. The legs should be short and as straight as possible, and the feet round and cat-like with thick pads. Colour is generally all white, or white with lemon, brown or badger-pied markings on head and ears. Measurements are not very helpful in appraising the merits of a dog, but the best height is from 8 to 12 in. at the shoulder.

Skye Terriers

DR Johnanne Caius, writing *De Canibus Britannicus* in 1570, mentions 'Terrars', one variety of which, he says were 'Brought out of barbarous borders from the uttermost country northwards . . . they, by reason of the length of their hair, make show neither of face nor body'. It would be nice to think, and it is not impossible to believe, that the learned doctor was referring to the ancestors of the Skye Terrier. On the other hand it has long been a legend that the Skye Terrier sprang from a little white dog who was washed up on the shores of the island along with the wreckage of the Armada. This little castaway would presumably have been a Maltese and if the story is true it must have mated with the native dogs. The story is given some support by the likeness of 'Quilick', the Skye Terrier used by 'Stonehenge' to illustrate the breed in one of his books, to a Maltese.

Undoubtedly the dogs of Skye were originally working dogs for they are described as creeping into subterranean burrows to rout out foxes, badgers, martens and wild cats. Such dogs could not have been as large or as profusely coated as the dogs of today; their coats were undoubtedly long, but they did not sweep the ground. When foxes became a menace to the island sheep it was the local practice for the tenants and land-lords to band together and appoint a warden who, with two or three couple of foxhounds and a small pack of Skye Terriers, would control the menace.

The rapid increase of interest in canine matters that took place in the nineteenth century probably did more harm to the Skye Terriers than it did to any other breed. For some unknown reason the breed hurtled into favour as a lady's drawing-room pet and a profusion of coat became far more essential than sporting ability.

The Skye Terrier made its first known show appearance in a class for Scottish Terriers at Birmingham in 1860 and a year later the breed had classes to themselves at Manchester. There is more than a suggestion that a spaniel cross was introduced about this time to produce the then popular black colouring as well as a silky coat. At this period the weight of a Skye was about 14 lb.—at the present time it is more usually around 24 lb.

Mr Pratt's 'Piper' was the most admired dog of his time and the one on whom the breed standard was based. The Skye Terrier was one of Queen Victoria's favourites and Lady Aberdeen was one of the most serious breeders and exhibitors at a time when it was not very usual for women to show interest in sporting dogs.

At the present time the Skye Terrier has lost all claim to consideration as a sporting terrier and he has simply become a fancier's dog, whose virtues are measured by the abundance of his coat. There is little wonder that he is the least popular of all the terrier breeds. One can only hope that one day his admirers may see sense and with careful breeding return him to a position where he can remember that he is a terrier.

140

DESCRIPTION OF THE SKYE TERRIER

The Skye has a short, close undercoat and a long, flat top coat. The hair on the head is shorter and softer than the body coat, and veils the forehead and eyes. On the ears the hair is overhanging inside, falling down and mingling with the side locks, but allowing the shape of the ear to be seen. The colours in this breed are dark or light blue or grey or fawn with black points. The head is long with powerful jaws, and the skull wide at the front of the brow. The body is long and low, with a level back, deep chest and well-sprung ribs; broad shoulders, short straight and muscular legs. The average height at shoulder is 10 in., and the average length from the back of the skull to the root of the tail, approximately $23\frac{1}{2}$ in.

141

Staffordshire Bull Terriers

IN the eighteenth century, and the early part of the nineteenth, there were dog fighting pits all over the country—several of them in London, at Southwark and Westminster. The supporters of this most unpleasant sport were mostly men of depraved taste whose liking for blood and cruelty was frustrated by the abolition in 1835 of bull baiting. There was a short period when fashionable young men patronised the pits and owned fighting dogs, but, on the whole, it was too unpleasant an amusement to appeal to anyone but the prize fighters and tougher elements of society. Of the rules for organised dog fighting and the methods of training the dogs the least said the better. The dogs undoubtedly showed up far better than their masters for they had a grim tenacity of purpose and immense courage, taking great punishment and even death without a whimper. The type of dog most often used was often referred to as a 'Bull and Terrier' and this seems to indicate that they were the result of a cross between both breeds—the Bulldog for courage, tenacity, strength of jaw and neck and the terrier for agility and aggression.

Public opinion slowly made organised dog fighting less and less of a reputable pastime, while the coming of the Victorian era brought about a more humane and considerate attitude to animals. Nevertheless, the author Rawdon Lee mentions a fight that took place as recently as 1902 when one dog was killed outright and the other died soon after, and there have been whispers of secret meetings being held behind the locked doors of North Country pubs more recently than that.

From the sullen, crop-eared and muscular dogs of the fighting pits have descended two modern terrier breeds—the Bull Terrier and the Staffordshire Bull Terrier.

Until about 1930 nothing much was heard of the pit dogs, although they undoubtedly existed in small numbers in northern England and around Staffordshire and some parts of Wales. They were also to be found in the United States. By and large these dogs minded their own business and that of their owner, but every now and then they might be absent from their homes for a few hours and return with a torn ear, a mangled throat or even did not return at all. Quite suddenly one or two sporting men and breeders of other types of dog began to take an interest in these dogs—three of the most prominent were Count Vivian Hollender, who was well known for his Bull Terriers, Mr Tom Walls, the actor and owner of racehorses, and Mr Joseph Dunn. In consequence of the increasing interest that was being taken in these dogs the Staffordshire Bull Terrier Club was founded in 1935 and, despite the disapproval of some people, 310 dogs were registered in 1939 and 1,760 in 1946.

Around this time the old plug-ugly was undoubtedly crossed with other breeds to give him more quality and here the Manchester Terriers appears to have played a considerable part. The two great names of the early days of the Staffordshire revival were 'Monty' and 'Nell' for through them came 'Fearless Joe' and 'Ch. Gentleman Jim'.

Too strong and intelligent to be allowed all his own way the well-disciplined Staffordshire makes an incomparable guard and companion, although the modern tendency to breed the dog smaller and smaller seems to be a pity.

DESCRIPTION OF THE STAFFORDSHIRE BULL TERRIER

The standard formulated by the original Staffordshire Bull Terrier Club describes them as smooth-coated dogs, standing about 14 to 16 in. at the shoulder. They should give the impression of great strength for their size, and although muscular, they should be active and agile. The head is short, deep through, broad in skull, and has very pronounced cheek muscles, a distinct stop, short foreface and level mouth. The weight for dogs is from 28 to 38 lb., and bitches 4 lb. less. The ears may be rose, half-pricked or pricked. Eyes dark. Neck muscular and rather short. Nose black. Body short, brisket deep, loins light, forelegs set rather wide apart to permit of chest development. Forelegs should be straight, feet well padded. Hindquarters well muscled and let down at hocks. Coat short, smooth and close. Tail of medium length, tapering to a point and carried rather low. Colour, any shade of brindle—black, white, fawn or red, or any of these colours with white.

Welsh Terriers

TO the uninitiated the Welsh Terrier bears a considerable resemblance to a small Airedale Terrier. These dogs were accepted as an individual breed only after considerable controversy. Harsh coated, black-and-tan terriers were to be found not only in Wales but in several parts of England especially the northern counties where they were known as Old English Broken-haired Terriers. There was nothing surprising about this for undoubtedly black-and-tan is a basic terrier colour. The Welsh claimed a chain of descent for their dogs that went back several hundred years; the North Country Englishmen were not nearly so well briefed in terrier history nor were they as vocal as the Welshmen. When in 1885 both parties met representatives of the Kennel Club, and the Kennel Club Committee finally agreed to classify the dogs as 'Welsh Terriers or Old English Wire-haired Terriers', the clumsy definition satisfied no one. The Welsh party were shrewd and got busy forming a club for 'Welsh Terriers'. The English Terrier faction failed in their effort to found a club for themselves and in consequence it was not long before the Kennel Club decreed that, whether of Welsh or English descent, all black-and-tan, broken-haired terriers would be designated Welsh Terriers.

Welsh Terriers have changed considerably in appearance since 1887, which was the year in which the first champion was made up. 'Ch. Dim Saesonaeg' was a dog of quite different appearance from the modern Welsh Terriers—he was of a more leggy, rangy build with an untrimmed coat and a pointed muzzle. Nevertheless, pictures of this dog show that he had a keen, alert terrier-like expression. His son 'Ch. Cymro-o-Gymry' appears to have been as dumpy as his father was lanky.

Mr Walter Glyn can be said to have been the real architect of the breed. 'Ch. Dim Saesonaeg' was his first Welsh Terrier, but far from his last, for a string of champions emerged from his 'Brynhir' kennels during the years that followed—'Banker', 'Ballad', 'Betty', 'Blossom', 'Bonnet', 'Brittle', 'Bumper', 'Burglar', 'Burner' and 'Burnish' among them.

During the first part of the present century there was more uniformity of type and the trimming of Welsh Terrier coats became an accepted practice.

On two occasions since the last war Welsh Terriers have won the most coveted honour of the world of dogs—Best of Breed at Cruft's Show—a somewhat remarkable feat since many numerically larger breeds have never achieved the feat at all. The first great occasion was in 1951 when Captain and Mrs I. M. Thomas' 'Ch. Twynstar Dyma Fi' achieved this highest of all honours and eight years later the dog 'Ch. Sandstorm Saracen', owned by Mrs M. Thomas and Mrs Leach, repeated the performance.

Welsh Terriers are, perhaps, too sturdily built for true terrier work; but they are game and fearless and definitely not pugnacious with their own kind. In consequence, they can be their owners' constant companions.

DESCRIPTION OF THE WELSH TERRIER

The Welsh Terrier's coat should be wiry, hard, very close and abundant. The colour may be either black-and-tan or grizzle-and-tan. The head is flat, and rather wider between the ears than that of a Fox Terrier. The jaw should be powerful, clean cut, rather deeper and more punishing than is usually seen in a Fox Terrier. The stop not too much defined. The V-shaped ears are small, not too thin, set on fairly high, and carried forward close to the cheek. The eyes are small, dark hazel in colour, and neither too deeply set nor protruding. Neck of moderate length and thickness, slightly arched and sloping gracefully into the shoulders. The back is short, well-ribbed up; good depth and moderate width of chest, and strong loins. Straight fronts are, of course, wanted and cat-like feet. Altogether, a sturdily-built dog weighing about 20 lb.

145

West Highland White Terriers

THE West Highland White Terrier and the Cairn Terrier are brothers 'under their skins' and started their public life as being the same breed of terrier except for the colour of their coats. That the darker coloured terriers, who became known as Cairns, appeared outside their native glens in larger numbers, is explained by the fact that the white and cream puppies were unpopular with many keepers and owners and, in consequence, went to a watery grave at an early age. However, the Malcolms of Portalloch and the Macleods of Drynoch thought otherwise and saved their light coloured puppies and bred from them with care and thus developed a white strain which Colonel C. D. Malcolm exhibited under the title 'Portalloch Terriers'. It is also notable that at one time Dr Flaxman had tried to popularise white Scottish Terriers under the title of 'Pittenweem Terriers', but pictures of his dogs show them as resembling West Highlands far more than they did Scotties.

It was in 1907 that the little white dogs first appeared in the Kennel Club Stud Book. One of the early show winners was 'Colonsay Calma', a grandson of 'Pittenweem King Kong'. Colonel Malcolm's 'Balach-a-Ghline' was shown at this time, but 'Morven' owned by Mr Colin Young was the first dog to become a champion. One of the earliest supporters of the breed was the Countess of Aberdeen who was interested in all the terriers of Scotland and whose father, Lord Tweedmouth, was famous as the earliest known owner of Golden Retrievers. Lady Aberdeen owned the famous early West Highland 'Ch. Oronsay'.

At first the West Highland White Terriers were greater favourites than the Cairn Terriers and there was a big demand for good stock from the United States. However, the Cairn Terriers suddenly came to the fore and left their white-coated brothers in the shade. It must not be forgotten, however, that the puppies of these two varieties were quite often literally brothers and sisters since they were freely inter-bred especially in Scotland. Inter-bred puppies were accepted for Kennel Club registration without question. The custom would probably have continued if breeders in the United States had not objected and ruled that such cross-breds were ineligible for registration or exhibition in that country. There was a great deal of stormy discussion in this country for the American decree closed an important market for British-bred dogs. Finally the English Kennel Club decided that inter-breeding between Cairns and Westies would cease on 1st January, 1925. Today people have forgotten that it ever happened.

The West Highland White Terriers have proceeded very happily without the support of their coloured relations and the breed has been fortunate in attracting the affection of several clever breeders—Mrs Cameron Head, grand-daughter of the Macleods, was one of the earliest and her Inverrailort kennel was very successful; then Miss Holland Buckley, now Mrs 'Winnie' Barber, founded her very successful 'Scotia' family, while Mrs Pacey's 'Wolvey' kennel has housed more than fifty champions of a breed that has both pluck and charm.

146

DESCRIPTION OF THE WEST HIGHLAND WHITE TERRIER

The West Highland White Terrier is not a white Scottie; he has a closer affinity to the Cairn, except in colour, which should be pure white, although it often has a creamy or yellowish tinge. He is strongly built for his size, which should be about 11 in. at the withers. Deep in chest and back ribs; a straight back and powerful quarters on muscular legs. The head is of the familiar foxy type and the jaws powerful. Ears small, erect, carried tightly up, and ending in a sharp point. Broad or large ears are very objectionable, nor should they be covered with much hair. Legs are short and muscular; the hocks bent and set well in under the body. Cow-hocks are objectionable. The tails, which are not docked, should be 5 or 6 in. long, and are carried gaily without being curled over the back. Long tails are disliked. The outer coat is of hard hair, about 2 in. long, and devoid of curl. The undercoat, which resembles fur, is short, soft and close.

147

NON-SPORTING

Alsatians   *Bearded Collies*   *Boston Terriers*

Boxers   *Bulldogs*   *Bullmastiffs*

Chow Chows   *Collies*   *Dalmatians*   *Dobermanns*

French Bulldogs   *Great Danes*   *Keeshonds*

Mastiffs   *Newfoundlands*

Old English Sheepdogs   *Poodles*

Pyrenean Mountain Dogs   *St Bernards*

Samoyeds   *Schipperkes*   *Schnauzers*

Shetland Sheepdogs   *Shih-Tzus*

Tibetan Breeds   *Welsh Corgis*

NON-SPORTING

'EVERYTHING that is not anything else' might well be a description of the breeds assembled under the somewhat misleading heading of 'non-sporting'. There is something slightly Alice in Wonderlandish about this canine group for it contains terriers that are not terriers and so-called spaniels who are too small to retrieve a sparrow. There are breeds whose ancestors were working for their masters when Norman William first set a foot on these shores and others who did not exist when the present century began and, in addition, many of them are extremely sporting.

Some of these dogs have long coats while others have short ones, some are large dogs, and some are smaller than others who are classified among the toy breeds. Some are natives of these islands while others came here from the United States, Germany, France, Holland, China, Tibet and the far northern hemisphere.

It is clear, therefore, that there is no definite pattern to make a bond between these varying breeds such as there is among the hounds, the terriers and the gun dogs, but it does include breeds that have interesting histories and some of the pastoral breeds who have always been of great service to mankind. Many of the breeds are in the highest favour at the present time while a few are going through difficult times or are still struggling for popular favour.

This non-sporting group is the largest and most rapidly growing of the five divisions arranged and accepted by the Kennel Club and one day it may be possible to sub-divide it and make the sixth section the working group.

Whatever the differences of size, colour, and characteristics of the breeds that make up this most important division of the canine breeds, they are all dogs with the virtues of their kind; if perchance they have vices, then man, who has so long been their master, must take a great share of the blame.

Alsatians

THE alternative but more accurate title of the Alsatian breed is German Shepherd Dog. In their present graceful form these dogs are not an old breed, but they descend from two earlier but much respected types of herding dog. It was in the latter part of the nineteenth century that the sheep-folding dogs of Wurtenberg were crossed with those of Thuringia. Obviously the object was to amalgamate the best qualities of the two types. The experiment was successful in that it produced powerful dogs with great intelligence: today they would be considered coarse and ungainly. Stories of a wolf cross taking place at this period have often been told, but it is very doubtful if they are true. Even if they were, would it be so shocking? There is nothing despicable about a wolf, but it is very doubtful whether the shepherds would have trusted a dog with wolf blood among their flocks, even though the work of the dogs largely consisted of guarding and keeping the sheep within bounds as they grazed the unfenced pastures.

By 1895 these dogs were of three easily recognisable types or strains—the Thuringia, the Wurtenberg and the Kröne—and Der Verein fur Deutsche Schaferhund was formed. Twenty years later this club had a membership of 50,000 and a good claim to be the world's largest canine society.

The first German Shepherd Dogs came to England in 1911 but made little or no impression. It was not until the years between 1914 and 1918, when so many Englishmen had to spend time on the Continent, that those who loved dogs observed the intelligence and sagacity of the German messenger, guard, and medical supply dogs. Inevitably some of these dogs came into English and American hands and aroused great interest in Britain and the United States as well as among those who served with the army of occupation. Before long the quarantine kennels of this country were overflowing with these dogs; the earlier arrivals mostly chosen more for love than their pedigree, but the later ones of a better standard, although German breeders were very reluctant to sell their best specimens overseas.

The shortage of first-class dogs, and the difficulty of obtaining them, handicapped British breeders badly at a time when demand was greatly in excess of supply and any long tailed, prick-eared dog or puppy could command a high price. Honest breeders fought a hard battle and by degrees British-bred stock improved and by the middle of the 1920s the imported 'Ch. Caro of Welham' and the British-bred 'Ch. Allahson of If' were the equals of any dog of their breed either on the Continent or in the United States. Then came the deluge! Many people believe there was an organised campaign to traduce the Alsatian breed and these dogs were accused of every crime in the canine calendar from sheep killing to treachery. Nevertheless, out of evil came good, as it so often does, for although the Alsatian tumbled from its heights of popularity the get-rich-quick backyard breeders soon went out of business.

One cannot keep a good dog down and the breed has climbed steadily upwards again, using stronger footholds, and it is now once more one of the most popular in both this country and America. There is not a dog more devoted to his master and his master's possessions than an Alsatian, but he cannot transfer his allegiance easily and if anyone undertakes the responsibility for a dog of this nature he cannot dispose of it lightly.

DESCRIPTION OF THE ALSATIAN

The ideal height for dogs is 24 to 26 in. at the shoulder and for bitches 22 to 24 in. Immense importance is attached to movement, which should be of the free loping gait of the wolf. Such a gait is only possible with well-placed shoulders and the various parts of the body in correct proportion one to another. The length of the body from the junction with the neck to the buttocks should be slightly greater than the height of shoulder.

The sides are flat, the necessary heart and lung room coming from the depth of the brisket. The head is long, lean and clean-cut, broad at the back of the skull and tapering to the nose. The ears, which are broad at the base and pointed at the tips, are carried erect. Eyes almond-shaped and as dark as possible. Legs perfectly straight with plenty of bone. The colour of the Alsatian is not in itself important.

151

Bearded Collies

THE Bearded Collie might well be described as old wine in new bottles for although these dogs are among the oldest of the British sheep-herding varieties it is only quite recently that they have appeared on the show bench. The term 'collie' is something of a misnomer. The shepherds' dogs are an ancient family and they and their work are mentioned not only in the Bible but by numerous classical authors. Through the years geographical conditions have had a considerable effect on the development of various types—the wild mountainous countries demanded strong dogs capable of defending their flocks against attack from wild animals, while those dogs who worked in cold climates had to have profuse and weather resisting coats for protection as they stood guard over their flocks at night.

In Britain the comparatively early elimination of wolves reduced the necessity for aggressive tendencies in our sheepdogs who have been expected to devote themselves more to herding their sheep than guarding them. The two British breeds who are true shepherd dogs are the rather mistakenly named Bearded Collie and the Old English Sheepdog. Both these breeds have profuse, harsh coats and round, strong skulls that contain a great deal of wisdom. Reinagle's picture of a Sheepdog reproduced in *The Sportsman's Cabinet* is very reminiscent of the Bearded Collies one sees at the present time.

No particular area of the British Isles has an exclusive claim to sheepdogs—where there were sheep there were dogs. When Mrs Willison wanted to revive the old type of Sheepdog it was in Scotland that she found the most typical of them and the best of all was 'Jeannie of Bothkennar' who is the ancestress of most of the Bearded Collies that are to be seen around at the present time.

Bearded Collies did not rush into public favour; several years elapsed from the time when Mrs Willison first interested herself in the breed, until there were a sufficient number registered at the Kennel Club for a separate register to be opened and championship status granted. It was 1958 when the first Challenge Certificates were awarded and the first of the breed to qualify was 'Beauty Queen of Bothkennar', a grand-daughter of the famous 'Jeannie'.

A breed never gets known and appreciated for its looks or its character unless it appears at dog shows, but only too often it then ceases to do the work for which it was originally bred. The Bearded Collie is no exception, but it has now found itself a very useful rôle in daily life and excels as a baby sitter, children's companion and family friend; in this rôle the dog has found great favour with a somewhat limited, but none the less enthusiastic, band of admirers.

152

DESCRIPTION OF THE BEARDED COLLIE

The shoulder height of dogs is between 20 and 24 in., and bitches between 18 and 22 in. The coat must be double, the undercoat soft and close, the outer hard, strong and shaggy, with the legs well covered all over. The colour is immaterial, though many prefer slate or reddish fawn. There is little hair on the nose, affording a contrast to the 'beard' which grows from each side of the muzzle. The Bearded Collie is very similar in conformation to the Scottish Working Collie. He is an active dog, free from stumpiness, and although strongly made is not clumsy or cloddy. The sharp enquiring expression is a distinctive feature of the breed.

Boston Terriers

THE Boston Terrier is an entirely American product with a good claim for consideration as the national dog of the United States.

These lively, intelligent little tailor-made dogs have a quite short history. There seems to have been no particular reason for mating 'Judge' and 'Gyp'. 'Judge' was a cross between a Bulldog and an English Terrier and 'Gyp', who also seems to have been known as 'Kate', is said to have been a small white bitch of Bulldog type. Since the year when this happened was 1870 and organised dog fighting was as popular on the other side of the Atlantic as it was on this, it is to be presumed that a litter of good game fighters was the first objective but this aim seems to have been forgotten quite early in the breed's history. A dark brindle dog with white markings, known as Wells' 'Eph', was the result of this mating and, in his turn, he was mated to the golden brindle Towin's 'Kate' about whom we know little. From these dogs practically all Boston Terriers descend.

These early dogs had a strong resemblance to Staffordshire Bull Terriers, although they were heavier in the skull and squarer in the muzzle. Known at first as 'American Bull Terriers' or more familiarly as 'roundheads' the time came when the supporters of this type of dog wanted to form a breed club. The very suggestion aroused the wrath of those who supported the true Bull Terrier and for some time the objection was supported by the American Kennel Club. In 1891 it was decided that, since the new breed had come into existence in Boston, it had better be called the Boston Terrier.

With such a mixed collection of ancestors it was far from easy to produce Boston Terriers of a standard type, or make a consistent improvement in the new breed. It was at about this period that French Bulldog blood was introduced and it was certainly responsible for imparting that intangible something known as 'quality' and without which no breed of dog is likely to find fame or favour.

Two big problems faced the breeders of Boston Terriers—the whelping difficulties that are inherent in all flat-faced bull breeds and, secondly, the necessity for perfect markings. These two handicaps have never been entirely overcome, but they ensure that the supply of good Bostons is never quite equal to the demand.

The British were unusually slow in adopting the Boston Terrier and it was not until 1927 that Mrs McCormick-Goodhart imported five dogs from Canada; it was another ten years before there were enough home-bred and imported dogs to justify the granting of championship status to the breed. The first champions were the bitch 'Ch. Unkansee Disturbers Pride' owned by the late Eveline, Countess of Essex, and Mrs L. E. Salmon's 'Ch. Massas Dollar King'. It was not possible to make further progress until the last war ended, since then the breed has justifiably and steadily gained in popularity both as a show dog and as a companion.

DESCRIPTION OF THE BOSTON TERRIER

The American standard requires that the general appearance should be that of a lively, highly intelligent, smooth-coated, short-headed, compactly built, short-tailed, well-balanced dog of medium station, of brindle colour and evenly marked with white. The head should indicate a high degree of intelligence and should be in proportion to the size of the dog; the body rather short and well knit, the limbs strong and neatly turned; tail short. The Boston Terrier's carriage must be easy and graceful. Stress is also laid upon the expression which, as indicating a high degree of intelligence, is an important characteristic of the breed. The top weight is put at 25 lb., and it is usual in America to divide the breed into the following categories: Light weight, under 15 lb.; middle weight, 15 lb. and not exceeding 20 lb.; heavy weight, 20 lb. and not exceeding 25 lb. Great importance is attached to the colour, and in the ideal the brindle pattern is evenly distributed throughout the body.

155

Boxers

SINCE beauty is but skin deep the Boxer would not have become so tremendously popular if he could not offer more than lovely lines, muscular strength and good colouring. The Boxer is gay, loyal, loving and brave but seldom unnecessarily aggressive, although he needs discipline and intelligent training if he is to give of his best.

The history of the Boxer is less than eighty years in length and the early chapters were written in Germany, although the first named ancestor of the breed was an English Bulldog called 'Tom'.

The Bullenbeisser is an old, rough, tough Continental breed descending from the Mastiff and approximating to our own Bullmastiff. A number of breeds have a touch of Bullenbeisser blood in their ancestry, but it probably stands out most clearly in the Boxer. It was almost certainly with the idea of refining the old breed, without losing its courage or tenacity, that a part Bullenbeisser-bred bitch called 'Alt's Schecken' was mated to 'Tom'. Of the offspring of this litter 'Flocki' is No. 1 in the German Boxer Club's Stud Book. There is, however, some mystery as to how the bitches to whom 'Flocki' was mated were bred and yet another unanswered question is why the new breed were called Boxers. The one certain thing is that the breed flourished and through a bitch called 'Meta von der Passage', born in 1878 (who was a grand-daughter of the original pair) came a line that led to 'Rolf von der Vogelsburg' who not only had an outstanding show career but, when the First World War broke out, was sent for training as an army dog and served with great credit. On his demobilisation at the age of eleven he won a final championship in the show ring. 'Ch. Rolf' left his mark not only as a sire but as one of the foundations on which the world famous 'von Dom' kennel was established. Herr and Frau Stockmann's kennel became famous in every dog loving country in the world and 'Damf von Dom' became the first German and American champion, while 'Sigurd von Dom' was one of the outstanding American sires.

The United States, less handicapped by quarantine regulations, fell for the charms of the Boxer and obtained many of the best German dogs long before this country paid much attention to the breed. It was only shortly before the Second World War that any interest was aroused in this country and 'Ch. Horsa of Leith Hill' was the only dog to have attained his title by 1939. German 'Ch. Zunftig von Dom' and the bitch 'Alma von Frankenwarte', who had just been imported, had an influence on dogs of the future, although 'Ch. Zunftig' was soon sent to America where he was sold for the benefit of the Red Cross. Nevertheless, he left a British-born son 'Stainburndorf Zulu', whose sons, mated to 'Alma', founded a wonderful line that had much to do with the tremendous Boxer boom that began directly after the war. Such popularity did little or nothing to help serious breeders who were aiming at quality before quantity, but at the present time matters have straightened themselves out quite satisfactorily and the Boxer breed is in a comfortable position about sixth from the top of the popularity list.

DESCRIPTION OF THE BOXER

The colours of the Boxer are fawn and brindle or fawn, sometimes with white markings. Height 21 to 24 in. at shoulder, average weight 62 to 66 lb. The body is muscular and lean, with deep chest, well sprung ribs and clean sloping shoulders. The neck round, of some length, gracefully arched and free from dewlap. The back must be short, broad, and strongly muscular. A characteristic of the Boxer is the pronounced stop, giving the head a distinctive appearance. Head must not be too broad, cheeks well developed and free from bumpiness, muzzle deep and broad with a dark mask. Length of muzzle one-third of total length of head. When looking alert, wrinkles show on forehead. Slight wrinkles on face reach from base of nose downwards. The tip of the nose lies somewhat higher than the root. Eyes dark. Tail docked.

157

Bulldogs

THE history of the Bulldog is far too long and far too packed with incident to be told in full here. The Bulldog may well be the national dog of England but his story is full of sordid and bestial incidents which make one prefer the dog with his courage and blind tenacity to his self-seeking and bloodthirsty masters.

The turning point in Bulldog history was the year 1835 when bull baiting finally became illegal after a long conflict of public opinion. For six hundred years bull baiting had been a favourite sport that is said to have originated in Stamford, Lincolnshire, where in 1209 William, Earl Warren saw two bulls fighting in the castle meadow. The butchers' dogs chased one of the bulls through the streets of the town. The chaos and the courage of the dogs so pleased the onlooker that he gave the field where the fight began to the butchers of the town for use as a common on condition that they found a 'mad Bull' on the day six weeks before Christmas for the continuance 'of that sport for ever'.

A bull baiting dog had a short life if he did not have strength, courage, tenacity and activity. The bull was usually tethered by fifteen or twenty yards of stout rope running from a strong collar to a stake driven into the centre of the bull ring. The animal was then infuriated by being prodded by goads and any other painful method that might occur to his tormentors. The dog or dogs were then released and carefully worked their way close to the infuriated beast awaiting an opportunity to get a hold on his nose or lip. An attack on the flank was considered a sign of cowardice. The bull would do his best to get his horn underneath the dog and toss him. If this happened the dog's owner attempted to catch him in mid-air and throw him back into the attack regardless of his injuries. The dog, however, once he had got his grip held on—in fact once he had got a grip and his feet were swung off the ground he could not let go since his own weight locked his jaws. Once the exhausted bull had fallen to the ground all the young dogs learning the horrible game were loosed to tear the flesh and get a taste of blood. The ideal dog was low on the leg so that the bull could not get his horns underneath his stomach, his neck and jaw were strong with the nose tilted back so that he could breath and yet keep his grip and the wrinkles of his face carried away the blood.

The origin of these dogs is fairly clear. A type of dog then known as the Alaunt is frequently mentioned and sometimes described by early writers. Probably the first reference to a 'Bulldog' comes in 1632 in a letter preserved at the Records Office in which an Englishman living in Spain asks a friend for 'a good Mastie dogge and two good Bulldoggs . . . Let them be good at the bull and cost what they will, but let them be fair and good curs'.

With the passing of bull baiting the dogs became to some extent redundant, although many were kept by tavern keepers and prize fighters. With the arrival of dog shows around the year 1859 the 'fanciers' began to exaggerate the points of the Bulldog to an absurd degree, but before long the breed had become a fashion on both sides of the Atlantic. The Bulldog has changed his old bull fighting character and become a pleasant and affectionate dog, with a nice character, but no longer able to take part in any form of sport.

DESCRIPTION OF THE BULLDOG

The head is a distinctive feature, with its wrinkles and deep indentations. The skull in front of the ears should be equal in circumference to the height at the shoulder. Between the ears the skull should be flat and not rounded. The jaws should be broad and square, the lower projecting considerably in front of the upper and turning up. The large nose should be set back almost between the eyes, which are wide apart; the ears, placed high on the head, should be small and thin, the correct shape being termed a 'rose' ear. The stout and strong front legs are placed wide apart, the development of the forearms giving them a rather bowed outline, but the bone should be straight. The hind legs are longer in proportion than the front, which gives the animal an awkward gait. The back, short and strong, needs to be very broad at the shoulders and tapering at the loins, making what is known as a roach back. A real roach, however, is seldom seen, and we have to be content with a pear-shaped body, tucked up at the belly. The stern is set on low and should be carried downwards.

Bullmastiffs

BULLMASTIFFS were frequently mentioned by nineteenth-century writers who often used the term 'Keeper's Night Dog' although, admittedly, not every 'Night Dog' was a Bullmastiff. There is, however, a wide gulf between the dogs of the last century and those who made their appearance late in the first quarter of the present. All the same, it is more than probable that the same breeds went into their make up— the Mastiff and the Bulldog.

The Bullmastiffs or Keeper's Night Dogs of the past were tough dogs. The common belief that the old time poacher was just a harmless, under-privileged villager who took the over-privileged squire's pheasants and rabbits to provide a meal for his half-starved family is far from true: more often they were roughs and toughs who worked in gangs and cost a number of keepers their lives. To preserve the game in their coverts a keeper or keepers often had to keep watch all night and they had to take steps for their own protection. The best instrument for the purpose was obviously a powerful and suspicious dog who had no qualms about using his teeth and, in the hands of men used to dog training, could be taught instant obedience. The old bull fighting stock made a good base from which to produce the sort of dog that was needed and the Mastiff cross added extra size, while Bloodhound blood was probably added to the mixture to improve scenting and tracking ability. On the whole appearance did not matter except that short, smooth coats of a dark colour enabled the dog to move more quietly and be less visible at night. Training simply consisted of teaching the dog to keep quiet when required, to attack on command or in defence of his master, and immediate obedience to the re-call.

The fame of these old dogs travelled down through the years to more recent times and so-called bullmastiffs were often employed as watch dogs and a Mr Burton used to give demonstrations with his 'Thorney Wood Terror'—a reward of £1 was offered to anyone who could escape from the dog who, although securely muzzled, would chase, trip and hold a running man until his owner ordered his release.

The public's interest in these excellent guard dogs led to a request that they should be eligible for registration, but the Kennel Club could not immediately admit a breed with such miscellaneous ancestors to its registers, although it did open a section under 'Any Other Variety' for 'pure-bred' Bullmastiffs; the criterion for 'pure-bred' was that both parents of a registered dog should be bred from three generations of Bullmastiff parents without the introduction of a Mastiff or a Bulldog.

Mr Moseley was the man mainly responsible for the evolution of the modern Bullmastiff in whose veins runs sixty per cent Mastiff and forty per cent Bulldog blood. Mr Moseley's 'Farcroft Fidelity', born in 1921, was the first of the breed to qualify for entry in the Kennel Club Stud Book. 'Fidelity' was the sire of the famous 'Ch. Athos' who is still remembered with affection by those who knew him, although they say wryly 'but he was a devil!' Dogs like that do not come today and obviously a Bullmastiff is too large and too powerful for every home, but when he can have space and adequate exercise as well as discipline, he makes a most charming and reliable companion and the most efficient of all watchdogs.

DESCRIPTION OF THE BULLMASTIFF

Breeders endeavour to produce a powerful, symmetrical animal, well-knit and active, courageous and docile, standing 25 to 27 in. at shoulder and weighing from 110 to 130 lb. for dogs, bitches from 24 to 26 in. and 90 to 110 lb. Coat is short and dense, colour any shade of fawn or brindle. Dark mask preferred. The head is large and square, with fair wrinkle. The circumference of the skull may almost equal the height. The skull should be broad, forehead flat, and cheeks well developed. Ears V-shaped or folded back, set wide apart and high, level with the occiput. Eyes dark and of medium size, with furrow between. Muzzle deep and broad and short. Moderate stop. Neck muscular, moderate length and slightly arched. Chest wide and deep. Ribs arched, back short. Forelegs straight, with good bone. Hocks moderately bent.

161

Chow Chows

THE Chow Chow has all the characteristics that once typified the Chinese mandarins of high degree—he is inscrutable, dignified, stand-offish with strangers, seldom actively aggressive but prepared to resort to stratagem to gain his own way, while his friendship, once given, is seldom withdrawn.

For all his oriental airs and graces the Chow Chow has never been much valued in his native land nor was he particularly carefully bred. The bitches were expected to produce fat puppies for the pot and in the northern districts the adults served as draught dogs or watch dogs and were sometimes used for hunting. Most Chows have long, thick coats and this was spun into wool while their pelts were often useful as leather.

In appearance the Chow is a typical representative of the Spitz family with his upstanding ears, heavy coat and tail that curls over his back. Two outstanding physical characteristics of the Chow are his straight stifle and hock joints which give him a stilted action and, secondly, his blue or black tongue and mouth. No one has ever been able to explain the reason for the latter peculiarity, but undoubtedly a Chow with a pink or patched tongue has a bar sinister somewhere on his pedigree.

The first mention of Chows in England comes about 1789 when two are described by Gilbert White in his *Natural History and Antiquities of Selborne*, although the name Chow Chow, meaning 'mixture', was not applied until far later. Two 'Chinese Edible Dogs' went to America in 1833 and nothing more is heard of them. In the years that followed the Zoological Gardens and Queen Victoria both owned Chows and in 1880 a bitch called 'Chinese Puzzle', who was probably a smooth coated Chow, appeared at several shows and was then never heard of again.

In 1887 the real history of the Chow in the Western hemisphere began. The Lord Lonsdale of the period gave a dog to Lady Harlech who passed it on to the Dowager Lady Huntly, who managed to acquire a bitch. This pair bred 'Peridot II' who was exhibited. With no quarantine laws to hamper importation, there was little difficulty in obtaining further stock from China, and the breed went ahead and multiplied with great rapidity. In 1894 the Kennel Club recognised the breed under the name of Chow Chow and by 1897 the first two champions gained their titles—the imported dog 'Chow VIII' and the bitch 'Leyswood Blue Bell'.

Appreciation of Chows appears to run in families, for the Dowager Lady Huntly's daughter-in-law, Lady Granville Gordon and her daughter Lady Faudel Phillips, all had a great influence on the breed and the 'Amwell' kennel owned by Lady Faudel Phillips was a power in the land. From the beginning of the century to the outbreak of the Second World War were the hey-days of the Chow breed and many magnificent dogs were bred and shown and numbers of them—perhaps too many—crossed the Atlantic. 'Ch. Akbar', the brother and sister champions 'Choonam Brilliantine' and 'Brilliantina', 'Ch. Choonam Hung Kwong' and 'Ch. Rochow Dragoon' and 'Adjutant' were unforgettable dogs, but since the last war the breed has never quite regained its high quality nor its position as a popular favourite.

DESCRIPTION OF THE CHOW CHOW

The Chow Chow is compact, short-coupled and powerful for his weight, which is usually between 40 and 50 lb. The head has a blunt appearance, the muzzle, of moderate length, being broad instead of pointed like that of a fox. The skull is flat and broad surmounted by small, pointed erect ears, that are placed well forward. This placement helps to give the scowling expression that is so much desired. Chest broad and deep; back short, straight and strong; loins powerful. Forelegs perfectly straight with heavy bone. Feet small and cat-like. In the hind legs the hocks are straight. The abundant coat is dense, straight and rather coarse to the touch, with a woolly undercoat. The colours are black, red, fawn, cream, blue or white. On the reds the feathering at the back is often lighter in shade. The tail is curled, and carried well over the back.

163

Collies

IT is by no means unusual to hear people speak of the 'Scotch' Collie. Although there are many Collies to be found north of the Border, Scotland has no proprietary rights in the breed.

Several writers of the last century suggested that the Collie was a cross between a form of sheepdog and the Scottish Deerhound or a Greyhound. This sounds most improbable for the instincts of the breeds are so contradictory: the age-old, innate impulse of the hound to pull down and kill anything that it has chased, by a hold on the throat or flank, would be most undesirable in a sheepdog.

The meaning or derivation of the word collie, colly or colley is far from clear. Shakespeare wrote of 'the collied sky' presumably meaning dark and clouded. Sir Walter Scott writes unflatteringly of 'a relay of curs called collies' and one wonders if the term described the same sort of dogs in 1745 as it did at a later date.

There are thousands of stories of the intelligence of the shepherds' dogs and the bond between master and dog but few descriptions of the dog's appearance. Nevertheless, there were undoubtedly dogs with a strong resemblance to modern Collies herding sheep in Wiltshire at the end of the eighteenth century.

By the middle of the nineteenth century Collies were no longer exclusively associated with sheep and shepherds: they had become aristocrats, popular both as companions and as show dogs. Americans clamoured to buy our most successful prize winners and long heads and long coats were soon worth long prices. The Collies of the show ring appeared to be an entirely different breed from the Collies of the hillsides, yet Mr S. E. Shirley's 'Trefoil' and 'Tricolour'—brothers from different litters—were the great grandsons of his shepherd's dog. A few generations of breeding for appearance had transformed the breed. It is more than likely that crosses with Gordon Setters and Borzois took place at various times—the former with the aim of producing black-and-tan dogs and the latter in the hope of lightening colour and lengthening heads. Neither of these attempts did any good, but did do some harm. The formation of the Collie Club in 1840 did a great deal to protect the breed against such experiments.

In their hey-day Collies commanded very high prices and 'Ch. Ormskirk Emerald', 'Ch. Christopher' and 'Ch. Sefton Hero' all changed hands for sums of over £1,000, which was big money in the early years of the century. By 1904 the breed was paying the penalty for success and one begins to find mentions of dogs with shy and suspicious natures; before long word went round that Collies were unreliable and treacherous and the breed inevitably faded into the background and others took its place.

At the present time Collies are staging a slight but steadily increasing 'come-back' to favour and, in addition, there is a renewed interest in the more uncommon smooth-coated variety. There can be no doubt that Collies are among the most beautiful of dogs and the temperaments of the dogs of today are far more reliable than they were fifty years ago.

DESCRIPTION OF THE COLLIE

Symmetrically built, Collies are active and enduring. Breeders aim at great length of head and profuse coats. The flat skull is moderately wide between the ears, tapering gradually to the eyes, and the muzzle is a fair length, but it should not be weak or snipy. The ears are small and semi-erect. The almond-shaped eyes are brown in colour, except in the case of blue merles, when they may be blue-and-white or china. The neck is muscular, powerful, of fair length and slightly arched.

The body is rather long, with well-sprung ribs, deep chest, and loins slightly arched and powerful. Legs straight and muscular, with a fair amount of bone. The outer coat should be harsh to the touch, and the undercoat soft, furry, and very close, affording protection against bad weather. Sable and white or tricolour are the popular colours, although the blue merle steadily grows in favour. The smooth Collie is identical in points except for his coat.

165

Dalmatians

THERE are almost as many marks of interrogation in the history of Dalmatians as there are spots on the dog's body. The one thing that appears to be clear is that the breed has no definite connection with Dalmatia, although there may be a link with Italy.

The suggestion that the Dalmatian may be of Italian origin rests largely on a painting of two typical Dalmatian heads by one of the Castiglione family and the fact that, under Cromwell's regime in this country, the breed appears to have been a symbol of popery. The latter fact, however, does make it plain that these spotted dogs were known in this country in the seventeenth century. In subsequent years most of the naturalists and writers on dogs appear to contradict each other, but the most interesting and enlightening remark comes from *The General History of Quadrupeds* by S. Hodson, R. Beilby and T. Bewick (2nd edition 1791), where it is stated: 'The Dalmatian or Coach Dog has erroneously been called the Danish Dog and, by Mr Buffon, the Harrier of Bengal: but for what reason it is difficult to ascertain, as its incapacity of scenting is sufficient to destroy all affinity to any dog employed in the pursuit of the Hare. It is very common in this country at present; and is frequently kept in genteel houses, as an elegant attendant on a carriage . . .'. That is a very clear picture of the status of the Dalmatian at the end of the eighteenth century and for quite a few years afterwards.

The custom of having a dog or dogs running between the wheels of a coach, phaeton or trap probably originated as a protection against highwaymen and continued because it made a pleasing adjunct to a smart turn-out. Dalmatians or sometimes Great Danes were usually employed for the purpose and the fashion lasted until the early part of the present century, when the coming of the motor-car made the practice impossible. There are many stories of the feats of endurance performed by Dalmatians and one notable dog is said to have done the fifty mile trip with the London to Brighton coach on eight successive days with only an occasional lift on his vehicle.

This contradictory dog, who has been credited with Dalmatian, Danish and Bengali nationality and said to be entirely lacking in scenting power, can, in fact, often be trained to be an excellent gun dog. He made his appearance in the show ring in the last years of the nineteenth century, when Captain Fawdry's 'Captain' and Mr E. T. Parker's 'Coming Still' were the notable dogs.

At the present time the Dalmatian may have had to resign from his traditional duties but he remains a very pleasant and level headed companion as well as a good guard. Many dogs of the breed seem to retain an inherited liking for horses and stable yards. There is nothing fancy about the Dalmatian, for his coat is short and close and easy to keep clean, while the clear black- or liver-coloured spots on the snowy-white ground are very attractive.

166

DESCRIPTION OF THE DALMATIAN

Dalmatians need to be strong, muscular and active, symmetrical in outline, and free from coarseness. The legs, of course, must be absolutely straight, with plenty of strong bone, and the hind legs should carry a lot of muscle. Feet round and tough. The head is a fair length; skull flat and broad between the ears, and muzzle long and powerful, with clean-fitting lips. The ears, of moderate size, are set on rather high and carried close to the head. Eyes bright and sparkling, dark in those with black spots and yellow or light brown in a liver-spotted kind. The neck, which is fairly long, should be nicely arched, light and tapering, and free from throatiness. Markings are most important in the show dogs. The spots, whether black or liver, should be as round and well-defined as possible and distinct one from the other, in size from a sixpence to a florin.

Dobermanns

LET us face it—the Dobermann breed has managed to attract some very unfavourable publicity during the past few years. The fault undoubtedly lies more with those into whose hands these dogs have fallen than with the dogs themselves who, from their beginnings, have been bred to be watch-dogs, guards and trackers. The breed originated in Germany, where a dog may be far sharper and quicker off the defensive mark than would be tolerated in this country, where we like a dog to give adequate notice of his intentions if they are in any way anti-social. A Dobermann can and should be trained as a 'one man dog', never kept in large numbers, and should be taught absolute obedience: thus he can be a splendid guard and companion to anyone who is prepared constantly to maintain strict discipline.

The history of the Dobermann is a short one and is given in a rather confused form in a book on German breeds published in 1928 by the Publicity Department of Der Deutsches Kartell für Hundewesen and should, therefore, be authentic, but the author is vague at times and not very free with his dates. From this account it would appear that Herr Dobermann of Apoldia in Thuringia was not only the town's dog catcher but the municipal knacker and assistant collector of taxes. In any time he could spare from these occupations he was a bit of a 'sportsman'. This seems to have been a synonym for poacher! The dogs Herr Dobermann acquired in his first capacity were often useful to him when he was off duty and seem to have become quite well known in the neighbourhood where they were known rather scornfully as 'Dobermanns' thus making them one of the very few breeds known by the name of their originator. In the same neighbourhood as Herr Dobermann lived a Herr Stegmann, who owned a large type of stalwart herding dog much used for controlling and guarding the cattle he imported from Switzerland and who travelled by road. These hard, strong dogs, who were probably kin of the Rottweilers, are believed to have been crossed with the dogs of Herr Dobermann—the story becomes a little hazy here! From now on, however, the picture is more definite. A businessman and breeder of terriers named Herr Otto Goller saw a future for these rough, intelligent types and bought up all the bitches he could find around Apoldia. Those that he did not think suitable for his purpose he killed. 'Suddenly', we are told, 'a revolution was effected' and the Dobermann emerged as a lean and graceful dog with a close, glossy black and tan, brown or blue coat with red markings. There was no secret as to how this transformation came about. Herr Goller, the terrier breeder, had made extensive use of the large-sized Manchester Terriers once so popular in Germany! The excellent noses possessed by the new breed may well have been a gift from some Pointer treasure trove of Herr Dobermann, while their strength and determination came from the old droving stock.

The Dobermanns gained much publicity for their work as police and guard dogs in Kenya, but it was in the United States that the breed found favour before it came to this country. In 1952 the breed first gained championship status and its popularity, gauged by the number of registrations, has risen steadily up to the present time.

DESCRIPTION OF THE DOBERMANN

The Dobermann is a dog of medium size with a well set muscular body, a proud carriage and a bold, alert temperament. The head is long and clean cut, and the upper part should be as flat as possible and free from wrinkle. The top of the skull is flat, with a slight stop; the eyes are almond-shaped, moderately deep set, with a keen expression; the ears are set on high, as small as possible, erect or dropped. The neck is fairly long and lean and proportionate to the whole shape of the dog. The ideal height at shoulder is 26 in. for dogs and 25 in. for bitches. Ribs are deep and well sprung; legs are perfectly straight, muscled and sinewy, with round bone, proportionate to body structure. The coat is smooth, short, hard, thick, and close lying, and the colours are black, brown or blue. The markings are rust red, sharply defined, and appearing above each eye and on the muzzle, throat and forechest and all legs and feet, and below the tail.

French Bulldogs

IT was about sixty years ago that French Bulldogs first appeared at English shows and caused more than a little spot of bother. The reason for this is no secret—the Bulldog who typified British courage, tenacity and strong, silent strength had been altered by breeders on the other side of the channel without as much as 'by your leave'.

British Bulldogs were expected to have 'rose' ears, the variety that fold inwards at the back with the upper or front edge curving over outwards and backwards. Here, to our horror, were small Bulldogs, sounder and more solid than any we could breed ourselves, but with upright or 'bat' ears, being imported from France. Patriotism and insularity promptly combined to make a fine old brew.

After the banning of bull baiting, British Bulldogs had become very respectable and were no longer solely the property of the rougher elements of society or would-be-dashing young undergraduates. As early as 1862 classes at shows were divided into those for dogs over and under 18 lb. in weight. The aim of some breeders was to produce perfect miniature Bulldogs. Early photographs show that these unfortunate little dogs had every possible fault—pop-eyes, rickets, weedy little bodies and were either the runts of litters or the results of systematic malnutrition, but there was undoubtedly a demand for these little deformities.

On the other side of the channel this matter of pygmyisation had been approached with far more intelligence, possibly by the Nottingham lace weavers who, when they had emigrated earlier on, had taken some of the lighter weight Bulldogs that they had always favoured with them. Another school of thought thinks that the Continental bull breed—the Dogue de Bordeaux—was skilfully bred down in size and improved in quality by French breeders. There was probably some truth in both stories.

In 1894 Mr G. R. Krehl, a well-known exhibitor of many breeds, brought several little 'bouledogues' from France and exhibited them in England. It was obvious that we had been beaten at our own game and that the French had produced a better miniature Bulldog than we could and the only thing any reasonable person could argue about was the bat ear. When the worst of the brou-ha-ha had died down the little Frenchmen were treated like poor relations, given a few classes here and there and generally frowned upon by all except those who wanted a smart, intelligent small pet who was far more lively than the little home-bred products. The newcomers were also given a warm welcome in the United States.

With a dogged determination worthy of their dogs, a certain number of breeders went on trying to produce miniature Bulldogs. The 'rose' ear and general substance continued to elude them and year by year, but quite unobtrusively, the neater, sounder, bat-eared and more active Frenchies gathered admirers; until in 1902 an uneasy situation ended with the French Bulldog supporters founding their own club and holding their first show and, before long, the little English miniature Bulldogs had simply faded away.

The French Bulldog is a 'character'—amusing, intelligent and willing to adapt himself to life in a London flat or a country cottage, and he deserves even greater popularity than he has already achieved.

170

DESCRIPTION OF THE FRENCH BULLDOG

The French Bulldog has clearly defined and distinctive characteristics, and is a smart, fairly active, clean built animal, with much that is likeable about it. Teeth and tongue should on no account be shown, as would be the case if the under-jaw was too prominent. The thick upper lip hangs sufficiently low to cover the lower as well as the teeth. The chest is wide, deep, and well let down; the back broad and short, forming a roach at the loins. The forelegs, set wide apart, are short, straight, strong and muscular; the hind legs, also muscular, are somewhat longer. Ribs well sprung; tail short, set low, and carried downwards. The coat is fine, brilliant in colouring, and soft to the touch. The most usual colour is brindle, but pied dogs (white and brindle) are most attractive and very much in favour. Black, tan or mouse-grey are serious faults.

Great Danes

G REAT DANES have little or no connection with Denmark, but owe a great deal to breeders in central Europe and Germany. The Great Dane descends from an amalgamation of the Wolfhounds, Boarhounds and Mastiffs who had been coveted by the Romans, valued by the Normans and subsequently utilised by all those interested in the chase.

Since large wild game survived in the forests of central Europe longer than it did elsewhere on the Continent, it is not difficult to understand why an agile and powerful hound, suitable for boar and even wolf hunting, should be popular in the castles and hunting lodges of the German princes and their followers where, until about 1880, they were usually called Ulmer Doggen or Hatzruden, although the great French naturalist the Compte de Buffon (1707-1788) is said to have been the first to refer to them as grands danois. Undoubtedly very similar dogs had flourished in this country for uncounted years, but by the nineteenth century the Continental type was more refined and better established.

From the middle of the nineteenth century enthusiasm for these dogs developed rapidly both in this country and in Germany where it was almost regarded as the national breed; nevertheless the English founded the Great Dane Club six years before the establishment of the German club. English canine writers of the period were not very kind to the breed and it had a further set-back when ear cropping became illegal. Hardly had breeders overcome the difficulty of breeding dogs with small, neat and well carried ears than the passing of the quarantine law made it difficult to import new blood. However, these difficulties were a challenge and British breeders were soon producing dogs every bit as good as those that could be seen on the Continent.

'Satan' and 'Prosperina', both owned by Mr Adcock, were two of the best known of the early Danes, and 'Cedric the Saxon', 'Leal' and 'Cid Campeador' were the largest dogs exhibited in 1885; their heights of $33\frac{1}{4}$ in. to $33\frac{3}{4}$ in. at the shoulder compare well with the size of the dogs of today.

In the years between the First and Second World Wars two kennels completely dominated the English Great Dane world. The 'Ouborough' kennel was owned by the late Mr J. V. Rank and the 'Send' kennel was the property of the late Mr Gordon Stewart. Both were large establishments founded on the best of our own and Continental blood lines, and no money or effort was spared to produce the finest stock. Both kennels were successful. Whether two such powerful and all conquering establishments would have ultimately killed all outside interest in the breed, one does not know, but the 1939 war reduced breeding to a minimum. When, six years later, it was possible to press ahead, the 'Send' kennel had been disbanded and competition was on a far more competitive basis.

The Great Dane is a dog that gives an impression of dash and daring; in character he is slow to anger, easy to discipline and, by virtue of his size and strength, a guard dog *par excellence*.

DESCRIPTION OF THE GREAT DANE

In spite of his remarkable size and strength, the great Dane should be elegantly built. 'Elegance of outline and grace of form are most essential,' says 'the standard,' and size is also necessary. An adult dog should not be less than 30 in. in height, and the minimum weight is 120 lb. Bitches may be 2 in. and 20 lb. less. The beauty of the dog is greatly enhanced by an upright carriage of the head and neck, and the expression must be alert, almost to the point of fierceness. The head is long with strong jaws, and, as the muzzle is broad and the skull comparatively narrow, the head seems to be of equal breadth right down. A fair measurement from tip of nose to back of occiput is 13 in. Ears should be small, set on high, and carried slightly erect with the tips drooping. The long neck should be well arched and free from loose skin; forelegs straight, with big bone and rounded feet, plenty of muscle on the hindquarters; stifles and hocks well bent; ribs deep and well sprung. Colours are brindles, fawns, blues, blacks and harlequins. A harlequin should preferably have black patches on a pure white underground, although blue patches are permitted, but no other colour. These patches, which are usually fairly big, are of irregular shape, as if they have been torn.

Keeshonds

THE Keeshond is one of the most handsome and most typical members of the Spitz family. He has everything one expects of a Spitz—a profuse coat, upstanding ears, alert appearance, a tail that curls over his back and the characteristic nearly straight hocks. The dog's character is also typical of his family—he offers a strong devotion to his chosen masters and an independence of outlook, a great sense of responsibility for the property on which he lives; together with a liking for young things, especially children. The colouring and shading of the coat is one of the breed's greatest outward attractions and the clearly marked 'spectacles', one of the Keeshonds' most outstanding points, give the dog its characteristic expression.

The Keeshond was originally a native of Holland and the Rhineland and at one time it was common enough for one or two dogs to live on the barges that travelled up and down the canals conveying valuable cargoes from the inland districts to the ports and vice versa. It is often said that the characteristic Keeshond habit of making himself as small as possible when at rest comes from having had to live in such a confined space. Certainly those Dutch barges could have had no better insurance against the theft of their cargoes.

The origin of the name Keeshond is uncertain, but the most probable explanation is the connection of these dogs with the Dutch Patriot party when they were opposed to the Orangeists during the period of political strife that simmered in the Netherlands at the time of the French Revolution. The term 'Keezen' roughly meant rabble and the Patriots were fond of applying it to their opponents who used the barge dog as their emblem. The small tokens bearing the head or form of a Keeshond that can sometimes be seen in Dutch museums are relics of the period.

The earliest wolf-coloured Spitz dog known to have come to this country was the companion of George III and can be seen in a painting attributed to Gainsborough and now in Windsor Castle.

Various 'Fox' dogs appeared at shows in this country from time to time; in Holland the barge dogs were seen at Dutch shows in 1891. But there is no record of any coming to this country until 1905, when Miss Hamilton-Fletcher, later Mrs Wingfield Digby, bought two puppies that she saw on the Dutch barges and brought them to England. But it was not until 1923 that descendants of these early importations, and of some others that followed them, were exhibited and caught the public eye. Two years later the Dutch Barge Dog Club was formed but soon changed its name to Keeshond Club. 'Black Bock' and a number of other Dutch and German dogs were imported and the breed flourished. The late Baroness Burton's dog 'Ch. Dochfour Hendrik' became its first English champion.

During the years that have passed since those first little barge dogs arrived careful breeding has produced dogs of more settled type and with more quality than those of their native country. English and American Keeshonds are probably the best in the world.

The Keeshond does not need as much grooming or attention as his profuse coat would lead one to believe, but there are few dogs more beautiful when in the full glory of a well tended coat.

174

DESCRIPTION OF THE KEESHOND

The Keeshond Club desires that the head should be well proportioned to the body, wedge-shaped when seen from above, and sideways showing a definite stop. Muzzle of medium length, neither coarse nor snipy. Eyes dark, with well-defined spectacles. Ears small, erect, well set on head, not wide nor yet meeting. Coat dense, harsh and off-standing. Dense ruff and well-feathered, profuse trousers. A soft, thick, light undercoat. The coat should not be wavy, silky or woolly, nor should it have a parting on the back. Tail tightly curled, a double curl at the end is especially good. Plume to be white on top where curled, with black tip. Straight forelegs, cream in colour and feathered. Hind legs straight, showing little hock and not feathered below hock. Feet cat-like. A Keeshond should move cleanly and briskly. The ideal height is 18 in. for dogs and one inch less for bitches. Colours: wolf, ash-grey, not all black nor all white.

175

Mastiffs

THE background of the modern Mastiff is of great interest and antiquity, but it is quite impossible to do more than take a glance at it in this limited space.

The Mastiff breed, which is usually credited with being descended from the huge Molossian dogs of Epirus, can be compared to a powerful and ancient oak tree whose acorns have produced a forest of other oaks. None of the Mastiff's descendants is quite as large, but all have the same steadfastness, courage, honesty and complete lack of guile that characterises the parent stock. The Bulldog, the Great Dane, the Bullmastiff, the Dogue de Bordeaux and numerous other breeds can claim the Mastiffs as kinsmen, while a number of younger breeds have, through the above breeds, a drop or two of Mastiff blood running in their veins.

The huge Molossian dogs were warriors pure and simple; their descendants, probably brought to these shores by the merchants of Tyre and Sidon, were not then considered to be nobility among dogs, but yeomen whose main purpose was to guard herds and property. Alfred the Great and Howel Dda, ruler of South Wales, both refer to 'big dunne coloured hounds' and it was in these terms that Turberville mentioned them seven hundred years later. In the intervening years the Mastiffs were frequently the subject of royal displeasure, for early royalty gave serious consideration to the preservation of the game in their forests and there was severe legislation to prevent dogs from hunting. Henry de Knyghton says that King John ordered the death of all dogs and Mastiffs in every forest in the kingdom; this may be an exaggeration, but it is a fact that 'lawing' and 'expeditation' were compulsory methods of preventing dogs hunting in the royal forest; these consisted of either cutting a sinew in the hock, cutting out the pad of one paw, or of cutting off three toes from the right front foot. The practice was continued until the reign of James I.

The Lyme Park strain of Mastiffs was famous for a number of years and descended from the bitch who watched over her master, Sir Piers Legh, when he was mortally wounded at Agincourt. A photograph of 'Warnla', the last of the Lyme Park dogs, shows an animal with remarkable similarity to the dog in Sir Anthony van Dyck's famous portrait of the children of Charles I.

Serious selective breeding of Mastiffs started about 1835, when Mr Lukey paid 'the high price of £40' for a brindle bitch which he mated to a dog called 'Turk', descended from the Duke of Devonshire's strain.

It is obvious that not many people can now accommodate a dog the size of a Mastiff, and since the end of the First World War the breed has faced serious difficulties. Luckily the outbreak of the Second World War was anticipated and several good dogs were despatched overseas. By 1946 the breed in England was in a precarious position with a very real prospect of dying out entirely. Thanks to the members of the Old English Mastiff Club, who formed a fighting fund and obtained eight adult dogs and bitches and some puppies from overseas, the breed was preserved. These dogs were mainly of British ancestry. Thus saved from extinction, the Mastiff at the present time is in a healthy position, producing young stock with the character and characteristics one expects in Britain's oldest breed.

DESCRIPTION OF THE MASTIFF

The modern dog is large, massive, powerful and symmetrical and, at his best, he can move with unexpected freedom. The head is broad and looks almost square, the lips are deep and pendulous and the ears small and thin. The chest is broad, causing the forelegs to be set wide apart and the body is extremely powerful. Great size is desirable as long as there is quality as well. Their intelligence and fidelity in alliance with their great strength make them ideal guards, which duties they take with great seriousness.

Newfoundlands

THE aura of sentimentality with which the Victorians surrounded the Newfoundland breed did it no real good. No dog or dogs could live up to the sort of reputations they were given, or be expected to be constantly plunging into foaming torrents to rescue an incredible number of blue-eyed children who, if accounts were to be believed, fell from banks or boats and would have been swept to early deaths if it hadn't been for a handy Newfoundland; a dog who dived into the water, took a firm grip on the back of their sashes, and carried them ashore! Landseer's painting 'A Distinguished Member of the Royal Humane Society' caused a furore and no one thought how much better it would be if children were taught to swim. Presumably they are taught at the present time and just as well, since nowadays one seldom sees a Newfoundland unless it is on its way to a dog show. So much for a breed that was favoured by Byron, painted by Landseer, was the subject of a poem by Robert Burns and of a paper read by Charles Darwin to the British Association for the Advancement of Science in 1844.

Despite all this it has never been generally agreed how the breed came into existence —it has been claimed that such dogs were the descendants of dogs taken to the land that was to become Newfoundland by the Norsemen somewhere about the year 1000. This theory was shot down by a statement made by Captain George Cartwright in 1792 to the effect that the Beothucks or aboriginal people of that desolate land had no dogs, were afraid of them and, if dogs had ever been there, they would undoubtedly have been eaten. The more likely and more generally held theory is that these dogs were the result of a series of purely fortuitous crosses of dogs available to the fifteenth-century settlers.

John Cabot sailed from Bristol in 1497, but has left no accounts of his voyage or of what he saw in his new-found land; the English began to fish in the coastal waters very soon afterwards and were joined by Portuguese and the French. Settlements grew up along the coast and maintenance crews remained there through the long winter months. It is inconceivable that they did not have dogs for company and for defence against wild beasts as well as for their assistance on hunting expeditions. In a record dated 1611 there is reference to the presence of a Greyhound and in 1622 there are mentions of Mastiffs. Those more seasonal visitors, the Portuguese and French, were probably accompanied by their dogs and it is well known that the Portuguese fishermen favoured the Cão d'Agua, who were trained to carry messages and nets from ship to ship.

By the middle of the eighteenth century one finds an increasing number of references to a large dog that is arriving in England from Newfoundland and is described as a 'bear dog'. On the whole the secret of the Newfoundland breed's greatness and charm is not in the purity of its breeding but in its diversity. Undoubtedly two entirely different types had emerged—one to become the Labrador retriever and the other the far larger, burly, heavy-coated water dogs so dear to our ancestors. The first two Newfoundlands appeared at a show in 1860 and 'Oscar' is the first dog of whom we hear by name. One of the several 'Cabots' who appear in the records was owned by the Prince of Wales and won at Islington in 1864.

Two wars have made Newfoundlands rarities in this country; the breed only survived by virtue of importations from Finland and the United States and the devoted efforts of a tiny band of admirers.

DESCRIPTION OF THE NEWFOUNDLAND

The Newfoundland is built on sturdy lines, giving the impression of possessing great strength and activity. He should move freely on his legs with the body swung loosely between them, so that a slight roll in gait should not be objectionable. Bone massive throughout, but not to give a heavy, inactive appearance. The chest is deep and fairly broad. Even his tail has a good deal of power in it, and serves as a rudder when he is swimming. When the dog is not excited the stern hangs downwards, curving slightly at the end, but when he is in motion it is carried higher. The small pendent ears serve to protect the orifices from water. The coat is flat and dense and of a coarsish texture and oily nature. The head is impressive, being broad and massive, with the occiput bone well developed. The muzzle is short, clean-cut and rather square in shape. At one time white and blacks were much favoured, probably on account of the publicity given to that colour by Landseer in his paintings. Now they are seldom seen, nearly all being a pure black.

Old English Sheepdogs

THE Old English Sheepdog is more often known as the Bobtail for the simple reason that it has no tail at all. Puppies are sometimes born tail-less, but are more frequently docked close to the body soon after birth—a habit that is said to have come down from the days when a curtailed dog was exempt from tax.

It is freely admitted that the modern Bobtail is a far more carefully coiffeured creature than his ancestors, but not many of the present-day dogs are expected to spend days travelling over rough roads and muddy tracks, moving sheep or even cattle from pastures to market or from market to pastures new. In the days before railways and lorries a man and his dog knew no other way of moving stock from place to place. It was but part of a sheepdog's work, for he had to range over hills and downs to collect his flock, sometimes separating it from the flock of another owner as he drove them through gates, into pens or where his master willed, receiving his orders meanwhile by almost imperceptible signal or faintly heard whistles. No dog and man ever had a better understanding than a sheepdog and his master, but there was seldom time for grooming and beautification and the dog's heavy coat simply served as a protection against the weather.

The Bobtail was never a native of any particular English district, although some have claimed him for the western counties. In fact, no one sheep-rearing district has a better claim than another.

It was undoubtedly the Bobtail's intelligence and great charm of character that first attracted the attention of those who had no particular interest in sheep. There is no more lovable or loving dog than a true Sheepdog who, despite his apparent clumsiness and his large size, is always most anxious about the welfare and well-being of all creatures smaller or younger than himself, and he is never happier than when rounding them up and generally keeping an eye on them.

At the end of the last century, and the beginning of the present one, the Old English Sheepdogs became one of the most popular of house pets and a constant competitor at shows. One of the notable bitches was 'Ch. Fairweather', born in 1898, who, like so many of her contemporaries, had one wall eye and one brown. In working dogs this peculiarity had always been regarded with some favour since it was believed that the wall or blue eye gave the best distant sight while the brown one was better for near sight. Today, eyes may be either dark or wall, but they must match.

The work of keeping a Bobtail clean and tidy is small in comparison to the reward of owning one of the most loving, clownish, but wisest of all the pastoral breeds.

DESCRIPTION OF THE OLD ENGLISH SHEEPDOG

Old English Sheepdogs are singularly attractive in their coats of grey, grizzle, blue or blue-merle, with or without white markings. Besides that, they are strong, hardy, and as active as kittens, and their intelligence is of the highest order. They are symmetrically built, being free from legginess, and there is a peculiar elasticity in their gallop. The skull, which is rather square, affords plenty of brain capacity. The jaw is fairly long, strong and square, and there is a stop between the eyes. A long narrow head is regarded as a deformity. Eyes may be either dark colour or wall-eyed. Ears small and carried flat by the side of the head. Forelegs should have plenty of bone, and should be dead straight. Feet small and round. Some puppies are born tail-less, but most require docking. Neck fairly long and gracefully arched. Body rather short and compact; ribs well sprung; brisket deep; loins stout and slightly arched, with hindquarters round and muscular. The profuse coat is of hard texture, not straight, but shaggy and free from curl.

Poodles

OW, when, where and why Poodles came into existence is a question many people have asked without getting an entirely satisfactory reply. It would appear that the Poodle has long been a cosmopolitan for one finds traces of the breed in England, Italy, France and the Lowlands from the sixteenth century onwards. In pictorial evidence the dogs nearly always appear in the traditional 'lion' clip that leaves the hindquarters bare except for leg bands and a pom-pom on the tail, while the forequarters are heavily coated except for the face and legs. This appears to indicate that these dogs were originally intended as sporting and retrieving dogs and that a heavy, wet coat on the quarters was an encumbrance to a working dog. The pom-pom on the tail and the traditional red ribbon bow that holds the hair of the head back from the eyes were both signals to a man with a gun that it was a dog moving in the undergrowth and not a bird or animal. The word 'poodle' itself is said to derive from 'pudel', a low-German word meaning to splash in water. Surely these signs all add up to a sporting dog.

The earliest Poodle we hear of in this country was the white 'pudel', 'Boy', the much-loved companion of Prince Rupert. 'Boy' had been given to him during his imprisonment at Linz in 1640. During the Civil War 'Boy' was accused by the Parliamentarians of being a 'dog-witch' with the gift of languages and prophecy. His accidental death at the battle of Marston Moor made a sad day yet sadder for the Prince and added to the rejoicings of his enemies.

During a large part of his career the Poodle has been known in various sizes and colours—the so-called 'Russian' Poodle was usually of a large size and black in colour, the Germans fancied the brown dogs, while the French preferred them small and white. In those earlier days particolours or patched dogs were very common as one can see from the picture 'Les Tondeuse des Chiens' (1820). The blue, silver, apricot and other coloured dogs are modern developments not at all approved of on the Continent. Until comparatively recently corded Poodles had their admirers. These were generally the larger type of dog, sometimes clipped but never brushed: the long hair was greased, stranded and twisted until it hung in long smelly cords that often dragged along the ground, adding nothing to the dog's beauty and much to his weight.

With the coming of dog shows it was the larger or 'standard' Poodles, many of them corded, who did the winning—'Ch. the Model', 'Ch. the Witch', 'Ch. the Joker' and 'Ch. Orchard Admiral'. The latter, a normally coated dog, was soon joined by others from the Orchard, the Whippendall and the Wolvey kennels. The final split between the corded and the curly varieties was not accomplished until 1903. At this time there was no division of the dogs by size, but interest in the smaller variety was growing fast and shortly the Miniature Poodles, who stood under 15 in. at the shoulder, were established as a separate breed. Even more recently the Toy Poodle of under 11 in. has turned the Poodle family into a trio.

A true Poodle, whatever his size, should be a sound, intelligent, sporting and attractive dog.

182

DESCRIPTION OF THE POODLE

The Poodle's head is long, straight and fine, the skull not broad and having a slight peak at the back. The muzzle is long and strong, not snipy nor full in cheek. There should be no signs of lippiness. The almond-shaped eyes are very dark, full of fire and intelligence. Ears long and wide, low set, and hanging close to face. Neck well proportioned and strong to admit of the head being carried high. Shoulders strong, muscular and sloping. Chest deep and moderately wide. Back short, strong and slightly hollowed, loins broad and muscular, ribs well sprung. Feet rather small and of good shape, toes well arched. Foreleg straight with plenty of bone and muscle. Hind legs very muscular and well bent. Tail set rather high, never curled or carried over back. Coat very profuse and of hard texture, very thick and strong, of even length, the curls close and thick, without knots or cords. Colour usually all black, all white or all blue, but all solid colours are accepted. *Poodle* (*Miniature*): should be a miniature replica of the Standard Poodle—height at shoulder must be under 15 in. *Poodle* (*Toy*): height at shoulder must be under 11 in.

Pyrenean Mountain Dogs

IT has been said that the Pyrenean Mountain Dog is 'almost too beautiful'. Others may think other breeds even more lovely, but no one can fail to agree that the Pyrenean is a very lovely creature.

The Pyrenean descends from the large dogs of Asia Minor, kindred of our own Mastiffs; these were imported into Europe by the Romans who made use of them for both watch and guard dogs. As the tide of Roman domination receded the dogs remained behind, developing in various ways in different areas.

It never has been the duty of the Pyrenean Dogs to herd sheep nor should they be referred to as wolf dogs or Pyrenean Mastiffs. The work of these dogs is guarding the flocks against wolves and bears. Protected from the elements by their thick coats and armoured by their masters with heavy, wide and spiked iron collars, these dogs were often left alone with their flocks for days at a time. Travellers in the mountains in a less sophisticated age have often described the happy relationship between man, his dog and his flock.

The well-known nineteenth-century writer 'Idstone' (the Rev. W. T. Pearce) records that when visiting the St Bernard Hospice the monks had told him that at one of the periods when the stamina and number of their dogs were dangerously reduced they had found it necessary to cross them with 'the Pyrenean Wolfhound', and it is notable that the double dew claws found on the hind legs of the Pyreneans are often to be seen on St Bernards.

Pyrenean Mountain Dogs were once familiar at the French Court—it is said the little Dauphin became so enamoured of the breed when he visited Barèges with Madame de Maintenon that he was allowed to take a puppy, whom he called 'Patou', home with him and thus set a fashion at the French Court.

General Lafayette is believed to have taken the first specimen of the breed across the Atlantic in 1824, but it was to be another hundred years before the breed became stabilised in the United States.

1845 is said to be the year that a Pyrenean Mountain Dog first came to England to be owned by Queen Victoria, but there is considerable evidence that one or two may have been here at least thirty years before that. Nevertheless, neither the early importations nor those made in 1865 seem to have left any legitimate descendants.

In 1911 Lady Sybil Grant went to considerable trouble and expense to import the finest dogs she could find in the Pyrenees, where they were already becoming scarce, but before her plans could develop the First World War hindered all dog breeding. In 1933 Madame Harper Trois Fontaines took infinite pains and trouble to import the best dogs she could find and among them was 'Kop de Careil', the Adam of British-bred Pyreneans. From this last effort the breed really became established in this country and not even another war did it any permanent harm. Pyreneans are certainly here to stay.

DESCRIPTION OF THE PYRENEAN MOUNTAIN DOG

Pyreneans should be of immense size, between 25 and 32 in. at the shoulder and the weight should be up to 125 lb. The expression should be keen and intelligent yet kind. Soundness should be of the greatest importance, the gait is distinctive and is usually described as rolling and ambling. The eyes should be of a rich dark brown colour, of medium size and set obliquely. The tail should be of good length, well plumed and carried low when at rest, and high over the back when alert. The colour is all white or principally white with markings of grey, badger or varying shades of tan. He is a serious dog, dependable and docile.

St Bernards

THERE is an aura of romance around the St Bernard and many people have muddled fact with fiction. Some suppose that there have been dogs in use at the St Bernard Hospice since the time of its foundation by Bernard de Menthon in 962. This story is founded on a picture of doubtful authenticity which hangs in the Hospice chapel and shows the Saint accompanied by a dog that bears some resemblance to a bloodhound or alaunt. There is, however, no mention of dogs in the Hospice records until 1707, although there is some reason for believing that they may have been there and at work a hundred years earlier.

The Hospice dogs seem to bear some relationship to the Sennenhunden of the Helvetian valleys who, themselves, descended from the large dogs left when the Roman tide receded. The Sennenhunden were much valued as draught, herd and guard dogs and the monks of St Bernard would not have had far to go to find dogs suitable for the task of helping them in their frequent and wearying task of searching for snowbound travellers and weary pilgrims who crossed the Alps on their way to Rome.

With the stock they found so close to their doorsteps the monks set about breeding powerful animals capable of working at high altitudes and who were intelligent, obedient and smooth-coated. The latter point is notable since most of the dogs we see today are rough-coated, but the monks originally found the heavier-coated dogs unsuitable for working in snow and often gave away puppies of the long-coated type and consequently it was these that were the first dogs of the breed to be seen outside their own terrain.

By 1665 the monks seem to have met with success in their breeding and training experiments, but even in the Hospice records the term St Bernard was not used to describe these dogs and the usual reference was to Alpine or Hospice dogs.

At various times the Hospice kennels have been weakened by disease, accidents and in-breeding and fresh blood has had to be introduced. Pyrenean Mountain Dogs and Sennenhunden were certainly used from time to time, but probably Newfoundlands and Mastiffs have also been tried.

The popular conception of a St Bernard dog as a large, sagacious animal perpetually trotting up and down a snowy alp with a little keg of brandy round his neck as he searches for weary travellers overcome by storm and blizzard is a little far-fetched. The monks have always used their dogs in various ways at different times. They have certainly saved many lives and 'Barry' is said to have rescued a prodigious number of people. The dogs have also been used to draw sledges, to patrol from the Hospice to outlying huts, and the foot prints of the dogs have helped many travellers to find shelter. Modern roads and transport have made the work of the dogs superfluous and they have mostly been transferred to other Houses of the Order.

It was 1815 when the first St Bernard came to England and part of his fame was earned by having his portrait painted by young Edwin Landseer. In 1862 the Rev. J. Cumming Macdona founded his kennel and the St Bernard has been with us ever since.

DESCRIPTION OF THE ST BERNARD

The expression should be benevolent and kindly. The head is very massive, the circumference of the skull being more than double the length. From the stop to the tip of the nose it is moderately short, and the muzzle is square. The lips are deep; the eyes rather small and deep set, of dark colour and not too close together. Neck long, muscular and slightly arched, with much dewlap. Chest wide and deep; loins slightly arched, wide and very muscular. Forelegs perfectly straight, with huge bone, and the hind-legs should not be cow-hocked. Feet large and compact. The minimum height of a dog should be 31 in., but the taller ones are preferred. In the rough variety the coat should be dense and flat, rather fuller round the neck, and some feathering on the thighs. The colours may be red, orange, various shades of brindle, or white with patches on the body. The muzzle, the blaze up the face, collar round neck, chest, forelegs, feet, and end of tail—white.

187

Samoyeds

THE Spitz group have provided mankind with some of the most useful working dogs—most of the draught dogs that are so essential to dwellers in countries that are snowbound for half the year. The Samoyed is the most handsome of the Laiki family—a large sub-division of the Spitz group—and the breed name is taken from a nomad people living north of the arctic circle in an area between the Kara and the White Seas. The Samoyeds are a gentle and intelligent people who used their dogs for guards, for herding reindeer and for pulling their sledges. Their dogs have always been well used and, in consequence, are naturally friendly, and in their native state they lived in their masters' tents and slept by his fireside. When the outside world began to penetrate a previously largely unknown region and take an interest in the dogs they found there, it was not easy to persuade the tribesmen to part with them since they were not only essential to their livelihood but were their friends and companions.

The Samoyed was rarely seen outside his own country before the beginning of the present century, but by now he is far removed from the dogs of the tundras. One of the first people to bring these dogs to this country was Mr Kilburn Scott who imported his first dog in 1889. Other dogs were imported later and in the years that followed the 'Farningham' kennel, owned by himself and his wife, became famous.

Some of the early Samoyed importations were not white. 'Sabarka' was brown and there were other variations of the white, cream or biscuit colour that have since become the favourite coat colour. One of the earliest of the white coated importations was 'Perlene'. Her pictures show that she did not carry the profuse coat we have come to expect on our modern dogs, but structurally she was very similar to the dogs we see today; an interesting point since she came of good working stock, as her ancestors had accompanied the Nansen-Peary expedition to the North Pole.

The more sybaritic life led by the imported dogs, and more selective breeding, increased not only the length of the dogs' coats but their own size and substance. One of the early importations who had the most beneficial effect on the breed was 'Ayesha'. She arrived here in 1910 and it is said that she never had a bad pup—and she had quite a number. Through 'Ayesha's' female line came 'Ch. Kara Sea', born in 1924, whose victories and prize-winning descendants are too numerous to mention.

The outward beauty and the pleasant character of the Samoyeds has found them admirers in all parts of the world, while British-bred Samoyeds have travelled far and wide. In this country the breed keeps its registration figures at a fairly steady level and would probably increase them if people realised that the sparkling white coat is not difficult to keep clean providing it is of the right texture.

DESCRIPTION OF THE SAMOYED

Breeders of Samoyeds aim at producing an animal standing about 21 in. at shoulder, weighing up to 55 lb. for males and 45 lb. for bitches, with a back of medium length, and broad and muscular. The stout, straight and muscular legs should be long enough to admit of great depth and breadth of chest, but not so long as to constitute a weakness. Hindquarters strongly developed, stifles well bent. Broad flat skull. Muzzle of medium length and tapering foreface. Erect ears. Dark eyes. Black nose preferred, but brown or flesh-colour permitted. Thick soft undercoat, through which grow the harsh hairs constituting the outer coat.

189

Schipperkes

THERE is very little definite information available about the ancestry of the Schipperke—some would have us believe he just arrived complete and ready to do his job. The Schipperke is a native of Belgium where he was for long years employed as a watch-dog and rat catcher on the barges and other canal craft. He could sometimes be seen doing the same alarm service on the horse-drawn carts. It has been suggested, and the idea seems quite feasible, that the Schipperkes were originally Pomeranians, a breed of German origin and by no means strangers to the bargees who travelled the waterways of Europe. Since the Pomeranian's profuse and long coat would be a handicap to a dog whose daily life and duties were such that total immersion in the canals and rivers was far from rare, a cross was probably made with some sort of terrier. Length of coat was thus decreased and ratting ability increased. One laudatory description of the breed says of these little dogs: 'He has also a great fancy for the company of horses and on this account was formerly employed as a watch-dog in coaches, diligences and carts when, sitting proud, attentive and fierce on the front or highest part of the vehicle, he seemed more at home than in any other position. He is a veritable demon at such vermin as mice, rats, etc.'

The Schipperkes first came to this country between 1870 and 1880. One of the pioneers of the breed was Mr G. R. Krehl, who was always keenly interested in introducing new Continental breeds to these islands. The new breed was greeted with some excitement since it was believed that the puppies were born without tails. This, however, is not entirely true; some puppies are born tail-less but the majority have to be docked in infancy and no vestige should be left. It is this complete absence of tail that gives the Schipperke the typical rounded rump so reminiscent of a guinea-pig, with an ample 'culotte' or breeching of longish hair on the thighs. Another essential physical characteristic of the breed is the mane—the ruff of hair, longer than that of the body coat, that encircles the neck and appears to rise when the dog is alert or excited.

At the turn of the century Schipperkes were extremely popular in this country and there were large entries at all the leading shows; there was also a big demand for stock for house guards and companions. The welfare of the breed was in the care of several clubs whose intentions were good, even if they were inclined to disagree with each other. The outstanding dogs of the time included 'Ch. Joppe', 'Ch. Flying Fox' and 'Ch. Fandango', all of whom left a mark on the breed through their descendants.

The Schipperke is nearly always a black dog, but coloured specimens do crop up from time to time—chocolates, sables and even white are accepted, even if not wholly approved of.

The main reason why Schipperkes are not as popular as they were is because they are apt to take their guarding duties too seriously and lift their voices too often—a pity for they are extremely intelligent, hardy, and perky dogs with the added advantage of being portable when necessary.

190

DESCRIPTION OF THE SCHIPPERKE

In appearance the Schipperke is a small, short-backed black dog, of an average weight of about 14 lb. The foxy head and upright pointed ears give him a smart appearance. The skull is broad rather than round; the muzzle of moderate length; little stop is perceptible. The small, dark eyes are more oval than round and not prominent. They should be full of expression. The neck is strong and full, somewhat short, broad at the shoulders and slightly arched. Round the neck the coat is erect and thick, forming a mane with a frill underneath. Shoulders muscular and sloping; chest broad, with deep brisket; back short, straight and strong; loins powerful; forelegs perfectly straight; hocks well let down, and thighs muscular. Feet small and cat-like. The hindquarters are finer than the fore, and the rounded appearance of the rump is accentuated by the closely-docked tail. Coat is dense and harsh, and well feathered at the back of the thighs.

191

Schnauzers

THE Schnauzer is a comparative newcomer to the canine breeds and one about whom a number of questions can be asked. Primarily, are they or are they not terriers? Several experts have opined that they are, and the breed as a whole certainly has many terrier characteristics, but that final authority, the Kennel Club, has decided that they are not.

The Germans, the Austrians and the Swiss must have the great share of the credit for producing the Schnauzer in his modern form. How they did it we do not really know and the originators are not ready to tell us in much detail. The most probable root stock is the old rough-coated type of German Shepherd dog, and one German author has hinted that the Poodle and various Spitz may have had a place in the evolution that produced the 'bear' Schnauzer once frequently seen in Munich, where the variety was popular with butchers and hotel keepers. To preserve and improve this coarse but useful breed the Schnauzer Club was formed. In an effort to produce a larger yet more refined looking dog with a shorter coat, crosses with Great Danes—mostly black ones—were introduced. The dogs of this period were larger than those usually seen in this country and were known as the Reisenschnauzer and they are still very much in existence on the Continent. It is the 'standard' and the 'miniature' varieties that are best known both here and in the United States.

It is unusually difficult even to put a date to these polishing-up proceedings, but most of the work was probably done between 1880 and the early years of the new century. As the years passed a dog named 'Riego Schnauzerlust' seems to have had an outstanding influence and his progeny were scattered widely over central Europe. This seems to be the period when some Airedale blood was added to the previous mixture. That the breed was sufficiently stable to arouse foreign interest is proved by the fact that 'Mampe von Holenstein' was sold to America.

When Schnauzers first appeared in England somewhere about 1920 they were received with enthusiasm and considerable interest. In 1924 the Duchess of Montrose imported 'Busserl von Gruner' and founded her 'Brodick Castle' kennel. Another importation 'Bruno von der Secretainerie de Chavalard' sired 'Simon de Chavalard' who became the first English champion dog.

Miniature Schnauzers first appeared in this country shortly before the last war and the late Mrs Langton Dennis imported several good dogs.

Schnauzers of both sizes managed to keep a foothold in this country during the war years, but they could make no progress and they were in a difficult position by the time it was possible to start serious breeding operations once more. But breeders worked hard and with the aid of existing stock and a few importations from the Continent and from the United States we have some very excellent dogs at the present time.

The Schnauzer of either size can be recommended as a good and honest companion —not quite so volatile as a terrier but game, keen and determined.

DESCRIPTION OF THE SCHNAUZER

The Schnauzer's coat is straight, hard, dense, and wiry, shorter on the ears, legs and paws. The head is long and lean without being exaggerated, eyes dark with bushy eyebrows projecting well over them. The jaws are strong and powerful, and are furnished with bushy whiskers and beard, which give him the strong, rugged appearance for which he is renowned. He has a deep chest of moderate width, and the length of the body is slightly longer than the height. The tail, which is set on high, is docked short. Colours are pepper-and-salt or black. Miniature Schnauzers are identical in appearance but ideal height is 14 in. or less.

Shetland Sheepdogs

THE Shetland islands specialize in the diminutive—their ponies, their sheep and their sheepdogs are all extremely small. It follows that the small sheep who provide the wool that is one of the staple industries of the islands require a small dog to be their guardian. The dogs, like all sheepdogs, had to have sense, initiative and the determination necessary to keep their charges from wandering into danger as they grazed on the seaweed of the shore or from invading the precious crops or gardens of the islanders.

When, early in this century, an interest arose in this island breed, it is understandable that enquiries were made about its history. The Shetland islanders, always busy scratching a living, had naturally kept no records and no pedigrees, and calmly accepted the fact that their little dogs had always been part of the island's livestock. There was, however, one romantic and interesting story told—that long, long ago, before any living Shetlander could remember, a strange ship had been wrecked and broken up by a stormy sea and the sole survivor was one little bitch who struggled ashore cold, wet and exhausted. One of the islanders took her to his croft, fed and warmed her and a few days later she rewarded him with five puppies. This little family of castaways were the stock from whom all the small islands' sheepdogs descended. There is nothing impossible about this story, although it is only fair to admit that a very similar story is told in Skye to account for their terriers. Another possible ancestor of the Shetland dogs is the smaller type of 'Yakki' or Icelandic dog, specimens of whom might well have been left behind by visiting whalers from Greenland.

In their homeland these little shepherd's dogs were called 'peerie' or 'toomie', Zetland dialect words meaning respectively 'fairy' or a collection of shepherd's huts. Shortly before the opening of the present century the peeries began to make an appearance on the mainland, usually taken there by deep-sea fishermen returning to their homes in Scotland or East Anglia; having no clear title, these little strangers were not unnaturally referred as Shetland Collies, but this was to result in considerable argument as time went on. The peerie was a well-established breed and bred true to type and size, but the breeders on the mainland made no secret of the fact that they used small Collies to improve the style and symmetry of what had previously been sturdy little working dogs.

In 1906 the Shetland breed made an appearance at Cruft's and, soon after, the Shetland Collie Club was founded with headquarters at Lerwick. Then a storm burst! The supporters of the then very popular Collies objected to their breed being associated in name or otherwise with the newcomers. Eventually a compromise was reached and Shetland Sheepdog became the breed's official title, but it was not until 1914 that the breed obtained full recognition. Today the Shetland Sheepdog, even though he resembles a miniature Collie far more than his ancestors did, has overcome many problems and is now in a well-established position as one of the most attractive of the smaller dogs in the non-sporting group.

194

DESCRIPTION OF THE SHETLAND SHEEPDOG

Some Shetland Sheepdogs do not measure more than 12 in. at the shoulder. Can be any Collie colours; the outer coat should be long while the undercoat is soft and close; abundant mane and frill and legs feathered. Below the hocks the hind legs are smooth. The longest tail should have a good brush of hair, and is carried downwards with an upward swirl at the tip. The flat skull tapers towards the eyes, and the muzzle is long and tapering. There is a slight stop and the cheeks are flat. Almond-shaped eyes, brown in colour, set obliquely and close together. Ears small, placed high and carried semi-erect. Neck long, muscular and arched. Body compact, level back with well-sprung ribs and strong loins. Chest deep, shoulders flat. Fore-legs straight, thighs muscular, and stifles well bent, giving a racy appearance.

Shih-Tzus

THE ancestors of the Shih-Tzu (pronounced Sheed-zoo) probably lived in the Potala or the other monasteries of Tibet until that country came under the domination of the Manchus. In 1645 the Chinese had invaded Tibet and then confirmed the Dalai Lama as supreme monarch, but there is no exact record of when the Tibetans began to send the best specimens of their little 'lion dogs' to the dog loving court of the Manchu emperors. These lively little gifts carried an implied compliment to the scholar emperors Ch'ien Lung and K'ang Hsi since there was a Lamaist association with the dynastic name of Maujusri, the god of learning, who was traditionally accompanied by a small dog, which could, if necessary, transform itself into a lion and become his master's steed. The compliment was undoubtedly appreciated, for the palace eunuchs stated that the emperors were constantly followed by their small dogs, and the imperial entrance was often announced by their barking, which was a signal for all servants to hide or avert their eyes.

The imperial ladies and the palace servants were keenly interested in breeding small dogs, and these little 'lion dogs' frequently appear in the Imperial Dog Book or Scrolls where portraits of the canine favourites and beauties were recorded.

The Chinese gradually changed the appearance of their dogs, shortening, flattening and deepening their muzzles and rounding their skulls.

The last known date on which the Tibetans presented dogs to China was 1908, when the Dalai Lama visited the Empress Dowager and made the presentation in person.

There is no proof that any of these so-called lion dogs had left China for Europe before the twentieth century, but it is just possible that they or their ancestors, the Apsos, may have had some connection with the lion dogs mentioned in European books of the seventeenth and nineteenth centuries.

For all practical purposes the history of the Shih-Tzus in Europe begins about 1920, when the late Lieut.-General Sir Douglas Brownrigg and Lady Brownrigg were visiting China and were greatly attracted by a small, hairy, black and white dog described as a 'Tibetan Lion Dog'. With some difficulty they obtained a little bitch of similar appearance for themselves. This was 'Shu-ssa'. Later 'Hibou', an older dog whose master had returned to Europe, joined the family. Early in 1930 Miss Hutchins, who owned two of these little dogs, 'Lung Fu Ssu' and 'Mei Mei', returned to England with all four dogs and 'Shu-ssa' had her second family while in quarantine.

At first it was thought that the newcomers and others that followed them were Tibetan Apsos, the senior branch of the family, and it was 1935 before matters were straightened out and the newcomers took the breed name of Shih-Tzu. Under the auspices of a newly-formed breed club, they progressed well and attracted the attention of dog lovers in several other countries. Handicapped by the war the breed did not achieve championship status until 1949. 'Ta Chi of Taishan' and 'Yu Mo Chuang of Boydon', both owned by Lady Brownrigg, were the breed's first two champions, 'Yu Mo' being a close relation of 'Hibou' and 'Shu-ssa'.

196

DESCRIPTION OF THE SHIH-TZU

Shih-Tzus are lively and alert with a distinctly arrogant carriage. The head is broad, round and wide between the eyes, and they may be described as shock-headed with hair falling well over the eyes. They have a good beard and whiskers and the hair growing upwards on the nose gives a distinctly chrysanthemum-effect. The eyes are large, dark and round. The large ears are drooping, and so heavily coated that they appear to blend with the hair of the neck. The nose black for preference and about 1 in. from top to stop. Mouth level or slightly underhung. Body between withers and root of tail should be longer than height at withers. Legs short, straight and muscular, heavily coated. Feet firm and well padded. The legs and feet should look massive on account of the wealth of hair. Tail heavily plumed and curled well over back, carried gaily and set on high. Coat long and dense but not curly. All colours permissible, a white blaze on forehead and a white tip to the tail are highly prized. Size about 11 in. at withers, but type is of the greater importance and considerable variation is permissible provided other proportions are correct and true to type.

197

Tibetan Spaniels and Tibetan Terriers

ANYONE interested in the mysterious land of Tibet, as well as in dogs, could discover a great deal of interesting canine history if they understood the language. Tibet stood apart from the progress of the outside world for so long; its major policies were so often dictated by China and the majority of the inhabitants were too busy scratching a living for themselves to pay much attention to their dogs or their propagation—if they earned their meagre keep they survived. In the numerous monasteries, as in the Potala itself, things were a little better, and it has been possible to trace four clear types of dog.

Firstly, the large, bear-like and often ferocious watch-dogs, undoubtedly of Mastiff descent and who may well link up with the huge hounds of Kublai Khan whose hordes overran eastern Tibet in 1253. Secondly, there were small, heavily-coated dogs whose purpose in life appears to have been to give the alarm at the approach of strangers and whose warnings could, if necessary, be followed up by the appearance of one or more of the Mastiffs. The best and most typical of these were to be found in and around the monasteries and the Potala itself. These were the 'lion dogs', numbers of whom travelled to China as gifts from the Dalai Lamas to the Emperors of China and the Imperial ladies and, in the course of time, developed into the Shih-Tzu. The little true Tibetans are now well known in Europe and in Great Britain as Tibetan Apsos.

The third variety of Tibetan dog is known to us as the Tibetan Spaniel, and undoubtedly also came from the monasteries of Tibet, where an interest was taken in its breeding and in retaining its purity. But one wonders whether at some time or other someone at the Imperial Chinese court may not have returned the canine compliments sent from Tibet with a pair or more of their charming palace dogs who became known to us in the Occident as Pekingese. The likeness between the two breeds is undeniable, although the little Tibetans have longer noses, smaller eyes and a less exaggerated length of coat. Comparison of these dogs with pictures of some of the early Pekingese to arrive in this country leaves one with but little doubt that the relationship is not only present but fairly close.

The Tibetan Terrier is another variety that has settled down and is now multiplying in this country. These dogs are larger and longer on the leg than the Apsos, but they are also very heavily coated and curly tailed. Whether they are, in fact, qualified to claim the title of terrier is another story, but they are gay and alert dogs who are as quick to defend their homes in this country as they were to guard the caravans they accompanied for vast distances in their native and often mountainous land.

All four of these breeds have been seen in this country and all but the Tibetan Mastiffs can be said to have taken out naturalisation papers and settled down nicely, and the Spaniels and Terriers have championship status. Various attempts to arouse an interest in the Mastiffs seem to have been met with misfortunes of one sort or another, but doubtless the day will come when they too find a niche in English homes.

DESCRIPTION OF THE TIBETAN TERRIER AND TIBETAN SPANIEL

Tibetan Terriers might be likened to small Bobtail Sheepdogs. The skull, of medium length, is neither broad nor coarse, narrowing slightly from ear to eye, not domed, though not absolutely flat between the ears. A marked stop in front of the eyes, but this should not be exaggerated or dishy. The length from eye to tip of nose is equal to that from eye to back of skull. Muzzle not broad or massive, but of fair substance. Nose black. Eyes large and rather round, neither prominent nor sunken, dark hazel in colour, set fairly wide apart. Ears pendant, hanging close to the side of cheeks, slightly rounded at the tip, not large or coarse. Forelegs straight, length of leg from withers to ground should equal length of back from withers to root of tail. Feet large and round, well furnished with hair between the toes. The dog stands well down on his pads, not up on his toes. Body compact and powerful, but not cloddy. Back short and straight. Tail of medium length, carried in a gay curl over back or slightly to one side, well feathered. Double-coated, the outer long, profuse and fine, but not silky or woolly; long, straight or waved, but not curled. Head well covered with long hair, falling forward over the eyes, and a beard on lower jaw. Colour white, cream, grey or smoke, black and particolour, golden and tricolours. In fact, any colour except chocolate. Weight from 16 to 30 lb.

Tibetan Spaniels are in appearance rather similar to the Pekingese except that the coat is not so abundant and the muzzle is of a more natural shape. The head is medium sized, slightly domed; the muzzle of moderate length; the eyes dark and medium size. The ears are of medium size, lightly feathered, carried dropped, slightly forward and to the side of the head. The coat is short and silky in texture, and the tail, which is set high and curled over the back, is lightly plumed. Colours are varied—golden, cream, white, biscuit, fawn, brown, shaded sable, red sable, black, particolour or tricolour. Height is about 10 in., and weight, dogs 10 to 16 lb., bitches 9 to 15 lb., but the smaller specimens are most desired.

199

Welsh Corgis

T HE Welsh cattle dogs seem to have kept their integrity down the years and there are numbers of people who believe that small, short-legged dogs with a great resemblance to the herding dogs of Wales and the Heelers of the north of England were the original dogs of these islands and in possession even before the arrival of the Romans. Herdsmen's curs were given a high value and exempted from tax in the Cyfraith Howel Dda. It has also been suggested that there may have been inter-breeding between those early Welsh dogs and those of the Norse invaders: certainly there is a resemblance between the Bu-hunds and Vallhunds of the Scandinavian countries and the dogs of Wales.

It is most improbable, in fact quite impossible, that the Welsh herdsmen should have kept an unbroken line down through the centuries to the Corgis of today, but it is clear that a small active dog with quick hearing and keen sight has always been required for farm duties in the hills—nipping the heels of recalcitrant beasts and then dropping flat so the ensuing kick shall pass over their heads, quietly following up the advantage and keeping the beasts on the move. That typical 'dropping' action is habitual with many Corgis of today, most of whom are several generations removed from their working ancestors.

The derivation of the Welsh word 'corgi' and its exact meaning have often been discussed and argued and several answers have been given, but on asking a Welsh speaking farmer's daughter the question, without any previous reference to dogs, the prompt reply was 'a cur or small dog'. It should be accepted that the term 'cur' has only acquired a derogatory meaning comparatively recently—basically it means any working dog that is not a hound.

Despite their presence in the legends and stories of Wales and their long and useful records on the farmsteads, Corgis did not make an appearance in the outside world or at shows until about 1925, but by 1927 they had classes at Cardiff Championship Show. 'Dewsland Smudge' is said to have been the first of his kind to have been exhibited on the English side of the border. Things then moved quickly, for by 1928 the breed had been granted Challenge Certificates, and the years that followed showed more steady progress. In 1933 there was a tremendous move forward—Cruft's Show held early in the year had the largest entry of the breed ever to have been made, but this record was soon beaten at another show held in October. In July of that year H.R.H. the Duke of York, soon to be King George VI, bought the puppy 'Rozavel Golden Eagle' better known as 'Dookie' and started a connection between the royal family and the Corgi breed that has lasted up to the present day, and gave it a great boost in public opinion.

In 1934 the Kennel Club officially allowed the two types—Pembrokeshire and Cardiganshire—to separate. The former is the smaller, tail-less variety that has always been the most popular. The Cardiganshire Corgis appear in a wider variety of colours, are somewhat larger, with much longer bodies and full-length tails. Both branches of the family make admirable companions—clean and clever as well as gay and gallant.

200

DESCRIPTION OF THE WELSH CORGI (CARDIGANSHIRE AND PEMBROKESHIRE)

In the Pembroke type we have a foxy head with a wide skull between the ears, which are carried erectly and point outwards. The jaw is of medium length, rather inclined to be snipy. Teeth level and square, rather large for the size of the dog. Eyes well set, round, and of medium size, hazel in colour. The neck is fairly long and strong. The chest broad and deep and well down between the forelegs. The body is of medium length. The tail is short. The ribs are well sprung and the hindquarters strong and flexible. The legs are short and as straight as possible, with feet oval and strong. The coat is of medium length and dense, the colour being red or red and white, or sable, or black-and-tan. The approved weight is from 18 to 24 lb., and the height should not exceed 12 in. at the shoulder.

The Cardigan differs in having a long tail. His total length from nose to end of tail is about 36 in. Very short legs, slightly bowed. The head is a foxy shape, the skull being fairly wide and flat between the ears and tapering towards the eyes, above which it should be slightly domed. The muzzle should measure about 3 in. in length. The eyes are of medium size and preferably dark in colour. The ears are rather large, carried erect, and set moderately wide at the base. The neck is muscular and well developed. The body is fairly long and strong, with a deep brisket, well sprung ribs and clearly defined waist. The feet are rather round and well padded and are rather large. The tail is of moderate length and set in a line with the body, not curled over the back. The coat is short or medium and of hard texture. Any colour except pure white is recognised. The height should be as near as possible to 12 in. at the shoulder, and the weight of dogs from 22 to 26 lb.; bitches 2 lb. less.

201

Index